Queen
ELIZABETH
II

A PHOTOGRAPHIC PORTRAIT

Queen ELIZABETH II

PHILIP ZIEGLER

Revised and updated edition

Frontispiece: Princess Elizabeth at Clarence House, July 1951. *Karsh*

First published in the United Kingdom in 2010 by
Thames & Hudson Ltd, 181A High Holborn,
London WC1V 7QX

First published in the United States of America in 2023 by
Thames & Hudson Inc., 500 Fifth Avenue, New York,
New York 10110

This revised and updated edition published in 2023

Queen Elizabeth II © 2010 and 2023 Thames & Hudson Ltd, London
Text by Philip Ziegler
Foreword © 2010 and 2023 Emma Blau

Art direction and design by
Martin Andersen / Andersen M Studio
www.andersenm.com

British Library Cataloguing-in-Publication Data
A catalogue record for this book is available from the British Library

Library of Congress Control Number 2022951088

ISBN 978-0-500-02635-9

Printed and bound in China by C&C Offset Printing Co. Ltd

Be the first to know about our new releases, exclusive
content and author events by visiting
thamesandhudson.com
thamesandhudsonusa.com
thamesandhudson.com.au

Contents

Publisher's Note 6

Who Was the Queen? The Role of Photography
in Defining a Monarch – *Emma Blau* 7

Introduction: The Meaning of Monarchy 9

I The Making of the Monarch, 1926–1952 16

II The New Elizabethans, 1952–1976 84

III The Middle Years, 1977–1996 180

IV New Millennium, Old Monarchy, 1997–2011 216

V The Final Decade, 2012–2022 244

Chronology 262

The Photographers 266

Index 270

Acknowledgments 272

Credits 272

Publisher's Note

Camera Press, the London-based photographic agency founded by Tom Blau in 1947, has been one of the world's leading picture agencies for over seventy years. In particular, it has a long and prestigious history of syndicating official photographs of Her Majesty Queen Elizabeth II. The first photographer signed by the agency was the legendary Canadian Yousuf Karsh, closely followed by other early photographers of the royal family, including Cecil Beaton and Lord Snowdon. Through its connection with these photographers, who were favoured by the royal family, Camera Press built up a close relationship with Buckingham Palace, which continues to the present day. In consequence, no other agency represents so many of the leading royal photographers, both past and present, hence the rich variety of work selected from its archives for reproduction in this book.

Who Was the Queen?
The Role of Photography in Defining a Monarch

Emma Blau, Photographic Artist & Curator, Co-owner of Camera Press

Queen Elizabeth II's relationship with photography, most notably through official photographs of herself, developed over more than ninety years. It is astonishing to realize that this period covered nearly half the history of photography. The Queen chose to be photographed by some of the leading portrait photographers of our times, making the pictures an important contribution to the history of portrait photography as well as a fascinating record of her public image.

The photographs reproduced in this book pose interesting questions about how portrait photography is used both to document a person and as a way to convey a specific set of meanings about that person to the viewer. All of these photographs are likenesses of the Queen at certain times and places. However, the pose she adopted, the clothes and jewelry she decided to wear, the setting selected, indeed the photographer chosen and the way they composed the scene, and ultimately which frame Buckingham Palace deemed appropriate for public release – all of these factors contribute to the way the audience reads any particular image. Our understanding of the Queen in this context is, in fact, a careful construct with its own visual codes. There is a great deal at stake here.

These images also reveal the changing trends in portrait photography: the formal studio portrait; the intimate, documentary-style picture; images showing the influence of fashion photography; and finally, contemporary photographs where, to some extent, all of these styles have been appropriated and accepted. Indeed, through these high-profile examples we can analyse and explore the history and role of portrait photography: the work of its key figures; what the medium can reveal about the person photographed; the assumptions of the viewer; how photographs can be used to influence our perception of an individual. They operate on multiple levels.

Early childhood photographs of the Queen were taken during a period when her uncle, the Prince of Wales, was expected to marry, have children and become King. When we look at the images with this in mind, the young Princess has perhaps a more relaxed air than in those that followed his abdication in 1936, when Elizabeth's ultimate succession to the throne became more certain. During the Second World War, the Princess's role as future monarch starts to be referenced more explicitly and we begin to observe an increased sense of duty and responsibility in her portraits, such as Beaton's picture of her wearing the insignia of the Grenadier Guards and Dorothy Wilding's photograph of her in the Women's Auxiliary Territorial Service uniform.

Through the later 1940s and into the early 1950s, the portraits taken of the Queen were rather formal and even photographs of the young family seem carefully posed. To a certain degree, the equipment of the period, such as large-format cameras and static studio lighting, necessitated this approach. But perhaps in a time of shortages and post-war recovery the public looked to the young Princess for a sense of sophisticated style as well as for images of a royal family that reflected traditional values. These latter photographs could almost be those of any other young couple of the era with their children.

Major public occasions, such as the Coronation, still demanded an imposing image but the 1950s also saw a move towards a more Hollywood movie-star glamour. This change of direction continued with photographs inspired by the fashion photography of the 1960s and 1970s. In the same period, technical developments and the impact of reportage photography led to a more informal and spontaneous style of royal photograph. Patrick Lichfield, who took many of this type of shot, had the added advantage of being the Queen's cousin and his pictures undoubtedly reflect this relationship. There is a feeling that instead of creating a representation, he had the opportunity to observe and record behind the scenes, making the Queen appear more accessible to her subjects. Although different in style, the photographs taken by Lord Snowdon, who was married for some years to the Queen's sister, Princess Margaret, also have a more intimate feel and range over six decades of Queen Elizabeth II's reign.

How, then, was the Queen represented in more modern times? For her Golden Jubilee in 2002, instead of following the tradition of choosing an individual photographer, Buckingham Palace asked Camera Press to assist in selecting ten different photographers to create a varied portfolio of images of the monarch. The result was an interesting combination of the formal, the relaxed, and modern-day stylized portraiture. This series reflects how photography as a discipline now encompasses many contrasting influences and perspectives, even when photographing such an established figure as the Queen.

With the Queen's advancing age, sittings for official portraits became less frequent and arguably required a more static – and therefore more formal – approach, but historic events such as the Diamond and Platinum Jubilees and her landmark birthdays continued to prompt new releases. Jason Bell's 2013 photographs taken on the occasion of Prince George's christening captured four generations of British monarchs for the first time since 1894, and so we start to see a greater emphasis on the future of the monarchy, which is further reflected in Ranald Mackechnie's group photograph taken at the end of 2019 to mark the beginning of a new decade. In addition, both of these sittings addressed (and may well have helped to shape) a public perception of the Queen in her later years as the 'nation's grandmother'.

For the Queen and Prince Philip's platinum wedding anniversary portraits, Buckingham Palace selected another Camera Press photographer thanks to our previous connection with their royal wedding in 1947, when Baron's official photographs were the first set of images to be released by the newly established agency. There is a warmth and intimacy to Matt Holyoak's 2017 portraits, which were received affectionately by the press as confirming the couple's long and devoted relationship. While moments such as these were milestones for the monarchy and for the Queen, they were also relatable life experiences that many members of the public could identify with.

An exciting aspect of photography is the opportunity to collate images long after they were taken and to view them in their historical context. Many of the photographs published here were released for circulation at the time and then filed away. It is only now, revisiting them in chronological order from the Queen's infancy to her nineties, that the fuller story of her visual relationship with the public emerges. This is even more pertinent when we consider that no more photographs of the Queen will ever be taken. Consequently, these images are now significant historical documents in their own right that will come to define Queen Elizabeth II's life and her role as Britain's longest-reigning monarch.

Many questions arise when viewing this collection of photographs. What was the Queen's intent with regard to how she chose to have herself portrayed? What do the images approved for release tell us about how she wished to be perceived? Was she conforming to or, in fact, creating our own expectations of how a monarch should be viewed? What cannot be denied is the enduring power of the individual portrait of the Queen. Since my grandfather founded Camera Press in 1947, the royal family, society and the photographic industry have all radically changed. Yet the fascination with the Queen, and photographic representations of her, remains. It is a testament to Queen Elizabeth II, and to the photographers she selected whose work is seen here, that this visual dialogue continues to intrigue and captivate audiences worldwide.

INTRODUCTION
The Meaning of Monarchy

Every year hundreds of thousands of visitors, many of them from overseas, flock to Buckingham Palace and Windsor Castle. Trooping the Colour and other such ceremonies provide a focal point for their visits – they enjoy the horses and the uniforms, the music and the pageantry – but they would still come even if no such delights existed. Nor is it the appeal of history that impels them: few of them would have even the haziest concept of the role that the royal family has played in national life over the last fifty years, let alone the last five hundred. They come because, behind those louring walls and blank windows, is the home of that familiar yet infinitely mysterious, remote yet omnipresent, British monarch. For seventy years, these were the residences of Queen Elizabeth II and her equally ordinary yet extraordinary family. It is the mystery and the magic that draw the world to their doors; it was the Queen – practical, diligent, a little dowdy, in so many ways unremarkable – who incarnated that mystery and that magic, maintaining the line that has ruled England for more than a thousand years.

The word 'monarchy' means different things to different people. Often it means different things to the same people. It exists at several levels, each one distinct yet all inextricably enmeshed into an entity that is anachronistic, illogical, in the eyes of some absurd, and yet one that manages to work to the apparent satisfaction of the nation. Its precise powers and limitations are a mystery to everyone, including to the monarch. That the monarch is the Head of State is a cliché that could mean everything or nothing. Even the most ardent monarchist could hardly conceive that it might mean everything, however; not even the most red-hot republicans could claim that it meant nothing – though no doubt they wish it did. The truth, unsurprisingly, lies somewhere between the two. Exactly where it lies is hard to tie down and varies from situation to situation, from moment to moment. But it is nonetheless real for being so elusive.

Formally, the monarch is the ultimate repository of power. Surprisingly few people realize that that is more than just a polite but empty formula. The monarch is Head of the Armed Forces, but no one supposes that the generals look to him or her for their orders. The monarch is Supreme Governor of the Church of England, but it is the prime minister who selects the bishops and the archbishops. Yet the monarch is not a cipher. It is all too easy to conceive circumstances in which the monarch's power might become not a convenient myth but a reality. Let us suppose that in a general election the two main parties won almost exactly the same number of seats. The monarch's constitutional duty would be to ask the leader of the largest party to form a government. Let us imagine that this leader could rule only with the acquiescence, if not the active support, of another party in coalition, and that the price of their support was a promise that his or her government would introduce and endorse a measure that could never win the backing of the cabinet, let alone the parliamentary party, or a policy that would inevitably involve them in the loss of many seats; the party leader would report to the monarch that he or she was unable to form a government that would survive more than a few days in the House of Commons. The monarch would then invite the leader of the second largest party to take on the task of forming a government. The leader of the second largest party would in turn approach the leader of the third largest party and ask for their support. The third largest party, seeing that at last they might be in a position to force through a reform vital to their interests, would also set conditions for a coalition. If these were not met, the leader of the second largest party would be forced to return to the monarch and say that there was insufficient backing to form a government.

What must the monarch do now? Should the leaders of all the parties be summoned to Buckingham Palace to have some sense knocked into them? Must Parliament be dissolved and a second election called, in the hope that it will produce a more amenable House of Commons? What is certain is that the monarch must stand alone, reliant on whatever advice may be given by the private secretary and perhaps one or two elder statesmen who are deemed to be above the pressure of party politics.

Nor is this the only way in which the monarch might be required to use the royal prerogative in a way very different from the docile rubber-stamping that is usually the monarch's role. On at least two occasions over the last sixty years, it has seemed quite likely that a prime minister would ask for a dissolution and a general election in circumstances in which the leader of the opposition felt that, if given a chance, he could cobble together a workable government. In fact, in each case, good sense prevailed – the Queen found herself spared the duty of making what would have been an awkward constitutional decision. Certainly she would have had to be very convinced that she was doing the right thing before she rejected the request of her prime minister for a dissolution. But her former private secretary Sir Alan Lascelles went on record as saying that, not merely does this facet of the prerogative still exist, but that she would not have hesitated to use it if she had felt it to be her duty.

To some, the fact that this real power still rests with the monarch seems deplorably undemocratic. From time to time schemes are propounded by which some group of wise old men and women would take over the powers still resting in the royal prerogative. But wise old men and women, however wise and old, are only human, and few if any can have avoided some sort of political entanglement in the course of their lives. The monarch is almost unique among the inhabitants of the British Isles in being above politics. From earliest childhood the Queen was taught, and fully accepted, that it was her duty to stand apart, to consider only the interests of the nation.

For every theoretician who feels that it is improper for the monarch to exercise such power, there are a dozen pragmatists who believe that the arrangement, anachronistic or not, works well, and that any substitute system would be no better and might be a great deal worse. Its proper functioning, of course, depends on there being a monarch of wisdom, moderation and common sense. It was the good fortune of the United Kingdom to have such a monarch for many years, and there seems no reason to believe that under the reign of King Charles the situation will change in the foreseeable future.

The argument can be pushed still further. There have been occasions in the last few decades in Europe where a brave and determined monarch has stood almost alone in the face of a threat to impose an undemocratic and militaristic regime. It may seem supremely unlikely that any British king or queen could find themselves in such a position. We can take comfort in the fact that this is so. But at the back of one's mind lurks the consciousness that this need not inevitably always be the case, that economic or social pressures might overwhelm the state, that a situation could conceivably arise in which the proper workings of democracy might be threatened by totalitarian forces. In such a case, one can find reassurance in the fact that ultimate power rests, however remotely, with an institution that is above the fray and that can be relied on to do its best to protect the constitution and the liberty of the individual.

It is mercifully improbable that the prerogative powers will ever be invoked. Even without them though, the monarch is a singularly important element in the workings of the British government. Queen Elizabeth allied common sense with vast experience. She appointed fifteen British prime ministers; as Head of the Commonwealth and Queen of fifteen of its member states she enjoyed a relationship with its leaders that no British politician could share. Successive prime ministers paid tribute to her wisdom and attested to the value that they attached to their weekly audiences. That is the sort of thing that prime ministers are supposed to say, and it need not be taken entirely at face value. But Harold Wilson, to take just one example, used to return from his visits to Buckingham Palace in a spirit of conspicuous exaltation; his meetings with the Queen got longer and longer, and his staff claimed often to have detected changes in outlook as a sequel to these conversations. The Queen was, he sometimes said, the only person with whom he could legitimately discuss affairs of state who was not after his job. Put even at the lowest estimate, she was someone with whom a prime minister could let off steam and share worries in the absolute certainty that confidences would never be betrayed.

* * *

Infinitely far removed from the concept of the monarchy as an important element in the government of the country is the royal family as soap opera. One tends to assume that this is a product of the last sixty years. After all, in 1936, when Edward VIII's relationship with Mrs Simpson was about to provoke a sensational royal scandal, not a word appeared in the British press until the affair had almost reached its climax. Another fifty years before that, however, the escapades of the future Edward VII provided an endless source of gossip among those in the know and, since he made remarkably little effort to cloak his doings, 'those in the know' comprised a far wider circle than those who knew about his grandson's activities. And Edward VII's great uncle, King George IV, was savaged in the gutter press in a way inconceivable a century later.

It was only in the closing stages of Queen Victoria's reign, as the monarch took on a mystic and almost mythological status in the eyes of her subjects, that the press became more deferential. Even if it had not been so disposed, however, its tools, compared with the present day, would have been conspicuously deficient. There were no cheap mass-circulation newspapers, no radio, no television, no internet, no paparazzi, no royal servants who thought it proper to make a killing by selling below-stairs tittle-tattle to the gossip columnists, no clever technicians to breach the secrecy of text messages and mobile telephones. The privacy of the royal family was secure: partly because the ethos of the day protected it, still more because the means of breaching it did not exist.

It has been argued, as will become evident in this book, that the royal family created the appetite for gossip about their private lives by inviting the cameras and the microphones in to record their activities. They believed that, if the people knew how they lived and performed their duties, their popularity would inevitably grow. There is some truth in this: one of the more noticeable phenomena of the reign of Queen Elizabeth II was the conscious effort on the part of the royal family and its advisers to reshape its public image. But the appetite for picturesque and preferably salacious detail about the private lives of the royal family would anyway have grown in a less deferential and more gossip-orientated age. As the range of targets grew and the techniques available for their study became more sophisticated, so the royal soap opera would have swollen in its popularity. Undoubtedly a risk was taken when the shutters were opened and the light of day allowed to fall on the activities of the royal family, but if they had been kept closed the risk would have been greater still. The shutters would in the end have opened willy-nilly and the light of day might have proved far less sympathetic.

Nor is it all bad. From the point of view of the national economy, the soap-opera element of the royal family is a most valuable asset. Time and again, surveys have shown that the royal family with all its appendages is the single attraction that draws most visitors to London. Those who question whether, in monetary terms, the existence of the royal family can be justified should not only make arcane calculations balancing payments made under the Sovereign Grant against the Crown Estate or consider the implications of making the monarch pay income tax. They must also take into account how many million dollars, euros, yen, accrue to the national economy through the flow of tourism, and how great the contribution of the royal family is in the compound of the historic and the romantic that brings the tourists to Great Britain.

* * *

What is perhaps the most significant element in the potent cocktail that composes the contemporary monarchy is also the most unquantifiable. It is now many years since the *New York Herald Tribune* noted, with discernible irritation, how 'no egalitarian American can understand' the way that 'the British crown binds together the British people'. Since then the British people have become more polyglot and racially mixed, respect for hallowed tradition merely because it is hallowed and traditional has been notably weakened, the most venerable pillars of British society – the Church of England, the British Broadcasting Corporation, even the Marylebone Cricket Club – have been mocked and pilloried. The monarchy has not

The royal family at Balmoral in 1953. *James Reid*

escaped its share of denigration. But still the Queen remained one of the few cohesive elements in what seems often to be a disintegrating society. Far more than any politician since Winston Churchill in the early 1940s, she embodied the spirit of the nation.

It takes some great occasion to reveal the continuing potency of the monarchical myth. The Coronation in 1953, the Silver Jubilee in 1977, the Golden, Diamond and Platinum Jubilees of 2002, 2012 and 2022, all followed a remarkably consistent course. Initial apathy, complaints about expense and wasted effort, a gradual involvement of the people, hectic turmoil in the final weeks and then extravaganza was the common pattern of all these occasions. The only surprise, perhaps, was that there were no surprises. So much seemed to have changed, there were so many cogent reasons to expect each successive occasion to be but a pallid reminder of the great royal fiestas of the past, yet when it came to the point all was as it had always been.

It could be said that the extraordinary public reaction to the death of Diana, Princess of Wales, demonstrated a dislike of the monarchy rather than a tribute to its continued potency. Yet it was only because she was who she was that Princess Diana gained such extravagant attention. She could not have done it without her beauty, her charismatic appeal, her electrifying capacity for connecting with other people, but it was because she was wife to the future king, mother to his destined successor, that she became the centre of the nation's attention. If anyone doubted the continued force of the royal magic, the crowds that surged around Kensington Palace and Buckingham Palace – sometimes indignant and hostile as they were – proved that the people were as concerned as ever. It may seem paradoxical to suggest that the moment at which the Queen's grasp on the nation's loyalty seemed most tenuous was also the moment at which her standing was most emphatically reaffirmed, yet no other mother-in-law in the world could have stirred similar passions among the British people. It was because she was Queen, because she was expected to articulate how the nation was feeling, that her apparent failure to do so caused such outrage.

Reiterated failures to respond to the popular mood could do serious, perhaps even irreparable, damage to the throne, but it would take much hard work and ill will on the part of the incumbent monarch. There is a latent force, a power of attraction, in the contemporary monarchy that would survive much indifferent management before it was totally eroded.

In the early 1970s the Queen started to do 'royal walkabouts' so that she could meet people other than officials and dignitaries. This one took place in 1973 after the opening of the new London Bridge.

To establish the existence of such a force is one thing, to analyse it another. Max Weber, that most intractable of German intellectuals, described monarchy as possessing a 'powerful, magnetic appeal ... to which men are somehow peacefully and affectionately drawn'. Such an appeal is no more susceptible to precise definition than concepts such as 'charm' or 'sex appeal'. Because it is attached to an institution rather than an individual, however, it is possible to establish certain constant features that recur throughout the ages. Two elements above all predominate in Great Britain's enthusiasm for the monarchy. The first is the appeal of the institution to the conservative instincts of most of the British people of every political persuasion. The royal family is at the least a symbol, at the most a guarantee of stability, security, continuity – the preservation of traditional values. It is considered to be a defence against extremism, against the erosion of family life, against the disintegration of society. In the exercise of its functions is to be found patriotism and national unity; by her example the Queen encouraged conscientiousness, industry, decency; the monarchy provides a rudder that has kept the ship of state stable and sailing in the right direction.

The second element, superficially dissimilar yet by no means incompatible, is the appeal to the romantic. At the lowest these are the delights of colourful pageantry and soap opera; at a higher level the sense of history incarnate, of the blood royal flowing down through generation after generation from the mists of antiquity. It calls for the most trenchant radicalism or peculiar insensitivity not to feel some thrill of excitement at the extraordinary link with the past that the royal family and their way of life represent. They are but flesh and blood, yet to all but a few of even the most sophisticated of their subjects some slight flavour of the supernatural hangs around their lives. Though we know that the monarch eats, drinks and otherwise conducts his or her physical life upon lines very similar to our own, the obstinate conviction lingers on. The monarch is not quite like us.

* * *

One instrument that has increasingly both undermined and yet reinforced that illusion is the camera. The insatiable intellectual curiosity of the Prince Consort ensured that he and Queen Victoria were quick to take an interest in the burgeoning art of photography and it was as long ago as 1842 that the first image of a member of the royal family was recorded by this new technique. Eleven years later the Queen and Prince Albert became joint patrons of the newly founded Royal Photographic Society and it was the secretary of that body, Roger Fenton, who was the first to be invited to take an 'official' photograph of the monarch.

The need to set up elaborate and cumbersome equipment if a recognizable likeness was to be achieved ensured that, for many years, any photographer of a member of the royal family had to be given formal permission in advance. The rule was quickly established, and still survives today, that all pictures taken in an officially sanctioned session had to be submitted to the Palace. Some were approved for publication in one form or another – even if it was only to be cut up for a jigsaw puzzle or used on a chocolate box – some were retained for private use, some were consigned to destruction.

Usually the criteria for selection related to the purpose for which the photograph was destined – a rather more grandiose image, for instance, seemed appropriate for distribution on a State Visit to Nigeria than on a more informal visit to the United States. Sometimes the subjects of the photographs had their own ideas about how they wished to see themselves. 'Her Majesty', Queen Elizabeth's private secretary told the celebrated society photographer Dorothy Wilding in 1937, 'suggested that the hair and the mouth should be represented in a lighter tone and the eyelashes removed.'

By the 1860s, the idea that photographs of members of the royal family should be mass-produced for public consumption had become generally accepted. Formality, however, was still very much the order of the day. A smiling Queen Victoria was a rarity; most published versions portrayed her in a mood of sombre, sometimes almost bilious, seriousness. It was not until after the First World War that a slightly more relaxed element began to creep into royal portraiture and even then progress was sluggish until Marcus Adams pioneered the use of soft focus to add a romantic flavour to his photographs of the young Princesses Elizabeth and Margaret Rose.

It was Cecil Beaton, however, who did more than any other photographer to humanize, even glamorize, the royal family. In general, photographers queued up to secure the much sought-after permission to try their hands at royal subjects; Beaton was one of the few who from time to time found himself summoned without any prior application because some member of the family – usually Queen Elizabeth – thought it was time that a new picture should be taken.

Queen Victoria in 1854. *Roger Fenton*

To get on to the list of photographers who were permitted to photograph members of the inner royal family could be a protracted and often difficult process. A high level of professional skill coupled with a reasonable degree of respectability in both social and moral terms was the minimum required. Sometimes other criteria were invoked. Once, at least, a photographer was recommended by a royal private secretary principally on the grounds that he had had a good war and had been gassed while on the Western Front (luckily he turned out to be good at his job as well). The great Canadian photographer Karsh was recommended by the private secretary in the Governor General's office in Ottawa. Karsh, the King's private secretary,

Sir Alan Lascelles, was told, was 'rather unprepossessing … but there is no question that as a photographer he is becoming world famous … He is regarded as in a very much higher class than people like Cecil Beaton or Dorothy Wilding.' Fortunately Lascelles already knew and admired Karsh's work; one of the most memorable of royal images resulted.

Photographs have played only a relatively small part in shaping the way that the British people perceive their monarch but they are still significant. Have they done their job? Has the public relations exercise waged on behalf of the monarchy made any real difference? Was it necessary? Is the monarchy today as secure, as relevant, as revered an institution as it was in 1952? If this book is to be more than a collection of striking and attractive pictures, then it will be because it throws some light on such questions.

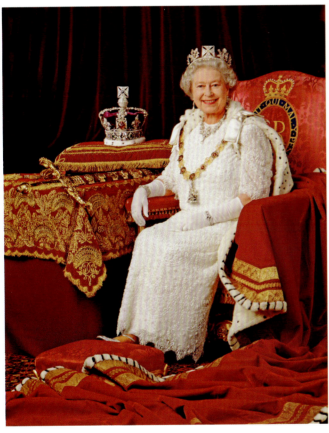

Queen Elizabeth II in 2001. *Julian Calder*

I

THE MAKING OF THE MONARCH

1926–1952

Like her great predecessors Queen Elizabeth I and Queen Victoria, Elizabeth II was not born to be Queen. Her father was a second son; when she was born on 21 April 1926 her uncle, the Prince of Wales, was only thirty-two years old, healthy, to a fault interested in women, and assumed by almost all his subjects to be likely to marry, settle down and produce an heir. Even if this did not happen, Elizabeth was a daughter: there seemed no reason to believe that her parents would not in due course produce a son who would displace her in the line of succession to the throne. She was not even the eldest grandchild of King George V; her aunt, Princess Mary, had already produced two sons, George and Gerald Lascelles. To say that her birth attracted no attention would be a travesty of the truth – the press and the public took an almost obsessive interest in the birth of a child to the Duke and Duchess of York – but the dread inevitability of the throne did not hang heavily about her cradle.

This is not to say that she had anything approaching what we would today consider a 'normal' childhood. Even by the standards of the British aristocracy of the time, whose children were brought up in remote nursery wings, cocooned by nannies and nursery maids, paraded only after tea and then having been duly washed and burnished for the occasion, Princess Elizabeth had an exceptionally cloistered and well-ordered infancy. The Yorks were in fact more preoccupied by their children

A family group after the christening of Princess Elizabeth at Buckingham Palace, 29 May 1926. Seated, from left to right, Lady Elphinstone, Queen Mary, the Duchess of York, Lady Strathmore and Princess Mary. Standing, from left to right, the Duke of Connaught, King George V, the Duke of York and Lord Strathmore.

than most young married couples of the upper classes, but royal duties and much related travel meant that they were affectionate yet inevitably remote parents. Her nanny, Clara Knight, always known as 'Alla', was a far more real figure to the baby princess than her own mother, let alone her dauntingly formal grandmother, Queen Mary.

Perhaps fortunately, Queen Mary was not the only grandmother. The Duchess of York, born Lady Elizabeth Bowes-Lyon (hyphens come and go with disconcerting rapidity in the Bowes Lyon family; no generation has been wholly consistent in the usage), was the daughter of the Earl and Countess of Strathmore. The Strathmores were Scottish aristocrats of immense antiquity, who considered themselves in no way inferior to their Hanoverian monarchs. Princess Elizabeth was born in their London house in Bruton Street, spent much time in their English home, St Paul's Walden Bury, a fine Georgian house in Hertfordshire, and passed much of her first summer at Glamis Castle, said to be the oldest inhabited house in the British Isles and formidably well endowed with ghosts, monsters and farouche towers and turrets. The Strathmores had the knack of being grand without being either pompous or pretentious. Queen Mary was as fond of her new granddaughter as Lady Strathmore and as concerned about her welfare, but in her mother's family Elizabeth found an informality and freshness that was hard to capture in the royal residences.

The first place she could properly call home was 145 Piccadilly, a substantial terraced house near Hyde Park Corner that was badly damaged during the Blitz and subsequently demolished. By contemporary standards it was enormous: five storeys, twenty-five bedrooms (including the servants' quarters) and a living-in staff of a dozen or more. The nursery was at the top of the house, well secluded from the Yorks' bedrooms or the grand reception rooms on the ground and first floor. Here Alla ruled supreme.

Until the advent of Marion Crawford in 1933, Alla was by far the most important influence in Elizabeth's life: strong-minded, kindly, intensely conservative, believing that regular habits and strict self-discipline were the prerequisites of a successful life. She was working in fertile soil. From an early age it was clear that Elizabeth was thoughtful, well-ordered, quick to take instruction and almost alarmingly diligent in the pursuit of what she conceived to be her duty. 'She is a character,' Winston Churchill told his wife, when he first encountered her at Balmoral in September 1928. 'She has an air of authority and reflectiveness astonishing in an infant.'

She had every opportunity to get to know her Strathmore grandmother since, when she was still less than a year old, her parents took off on a tour of New Zealand and Australia. The possibility that she might go too was not even considered; she was deposited at St Paul's Walden Bury. With no aeroplanes available to speed the journeys, expeditions of this kind were protracted undertakings and it was six months before the Yorks returned to England. Meanwhile their daughter had spent time not only with the Strathmores but also with King George V and Queen Mary at Buckingham Palace and Windsor Castle. Her contacts with her royal grandparents were even more remote than they had been with her father and mother, but she was regularly paraded after tea and the King reported dutifully to the Princess's parents on the number of her teeth and other signs of progress.

The Yorks with their children at St Paul's Cathedral for the Silver Jubilee service of King George V in May 1935.

The Yorks' second child, Margaret Rose, was born at Glamis in August 1930. The Prince of Wales seemed no more of a mind to marry and the possibility that Elizabeth might eventually find herself on the throne became each year more apparent. She had never been out of the public eye, but her sister's birth gave the York family a new prominence. Elizabeth's first full-scale biography – a work unsurprisingly lacking in substance – was not published until she was twelve years old but the newspapers, so far as they were able, followed her doings with avid sycophancy. Almost immediately dogs and horses began to appear in the coverage. Since animals were usually photogenic and added an agreeably informal touch to any account of the royal family, they would probably have featured even if Elizabeth had provided no reason for their presence. In fact, first labradors and then corgis played a large part in her childhood, while horses – toy horses, rocking horses, Shetland ponies, her father's hunters, the King's racehorses – became a passion that provided her most absorbing recreation throughout her life.

The arrival of Marion Crawford should have heralded a new phase in Elizabeth's education. Up to a point it did: 'Crawfie' did her best to inculcate the rudiments of the more obvious academic disciplines into her charges. But she was intellectually incurious, aesthetically blinkered, and determined that the two princesses should grow up happy, healthy and, in due course, good wives within the parameters of upper-class society. At one time there was talk of sending Princess Elizabeth to school but nobody could be sure whom she would meet there; appalling idea, she might become a bluestocking; better not. In time her French was to be taken in hand – with excellent results – by a Belgian émigrée and for extra history lessons she was assigned to the Vice-Provost of Eton, Henry Marten, but though Queen Mary made occasional efforts to widen her granddaughter's horizons, little was achieved. Elizabeth by 1936 was obviously no fool and showed rock-like common sense, but intellectual aspirations were denied her.

In that year everything changed. The Prince of Wales and the Duke of York had once been very close, but they had grown apart since the post-war years. The regular visits that the Prince of Wales used to pay to his nieces' nursery had fallen away and, since the advent of Mrs Simpson, had ended altogether. With the death of George V in January 1936 Britain had a new King, who seemed determined to consign all the old shibboleths to the scrap-yard and create a smart new-model monarchy in his own image. The Yorks watched this process with much distress, but this was as nothing to their horror when, ten months later, the abdication crisis burst on an unprepared nation. Determined to marry a twice-divorced American, Edward VIII renounced the throne and left it to his brother to salvage what he could from the wreckage. As the crowds gathered to shout their support outside the Yorks' London home, Elizabeth realized that something of profound importance to her family and to the nation was taking place. 'Does that mean that you are going to be Queen?' asked her sister. 'Yes, I suppose it does,' she replied. In fact it was not yet inevitable: the newly elevated Queen Elizabeth was still only thirty-six and there were rumours at the time of the Coronation that she was pregnant. A son could still have been born to claim the throne. But even then it seemed unlikely. From the moment that Edward VIII abdicated, shades of the prison house began to close about the future Queen.

King George VI and Queen Elizabeth with the royal children after the Coronation on 12 May 1937. *Dorothy Wilding*

The new King George VI was convinced that the scandal of the abdication and the disappearance of his much-loved elder brother would strike a fearsome, perhaps even fatal, blow at the institution of monarchy. In fact the nation shrugged off the loss of its King with remarkable equanimity, but George VI knew that he had neither his brother's quick wits nor his electrifying charm. He had, however, one trump card. How far a conscious decision was made to promote something that was anyway very close to the King's heart can never be determined, but, whether by chance or by policy, this is what happened. The picture of a devoted and smiling family was projected in innumerable variants and presented, both explicitly and implicitly, as the symbol of a national or, still wider, imperial family.

Most immediately, her father's accession to the throne meant a move from the cosy and relatively humble home that Elizabeth had grown to love to the dismal barracks at the end of the Mall. More importantly, it meant that more than ever she became the focus of popular attention. She was already used to playing a part on the national stage; now a starring role was thrust on her. The King and Queen realized the pressure that this must bring on even the most level-headed of girls. They made some efforts to broaden her circle of acquaintance and to make her life in some way approximate to that of an ordinary child. A Girl Guide company was established in the Palace and met once a week to practise its arcane activities. It was hardly representative of the movement as a whole – most of its members were the children of courtiers or aristocratic friends of the royal family, and the Kingfisher patrol, of which Elizabeth was second-in-command, was in the charge of her cousin Patricia Mountbatten – but it was still a great deal better than nothing. Elizabeth seems to have enjoyed it greatly.

How this initiative might have been followed up will never be known; in September 1939 Britain went to war. The nation had been taught to expect immediate and devastating attack from the air; in fact nothing happened, but the princesses were sent first to Scotland and then early in 1940 to Windsor, where it was felt that they would be relatively safe. Ministers suggested that they would be safer still if they left the country – perhaps to Canada. Queen Elizabeth memorably dismissed the proposal out of hand: the children would not go without her, she would never leave the King, and nothing would drive the King from his realm. Instead the princesses found themselves enlisted in the great propaganda machine working to boost the morale of the nation through years of privation and possible defeat. Repeatedly they were photographed diligently tilling their allotment, knitting scarves for the troops, engaged in stirrup-pump drill.

In October 1940 Elizabeth delivered her first broadcast, directed at British children separated from their families and forced to live overseas. 'My sister Margaret Rose and I feel so much for you,' she said, 'as we know from experience what it means to be away from those we love most of all.' The words were unremarkable; her voice, though clear and precise, could have been that of any other girl of her age; but the total effect was singularly moving. The little princesses were seen to be sharing the nation's suffering, solid in adversity, confident of final victory: 'We know, every one of us, that in the end all will be well.'

Princess Elizabeth tinkering with an engine during her ATS training at No. 1 Mechanical Transport Training Centre, April 1945.

It would have been much easier for the King if his daughter could have remained fourteen for ever, but when she came of age in April 1944 some important decisions had to be made about her future. Any possibility that Britain might be invaded and the war lost was by then over, but London was still the target of sporadic air attacks and those in the know were well aware that the onslaught of the V1s and V2s was not far ahead. Should the eighteen-year-old Elizabeth continue to be sequestered at Windsor or should she be allowed, like any other citizen, to play a full part in the war? The Princess herself had no doubts on the matter; she wanted to join the armed forces and do her bit. The King was uncertain: he saw the propaganda value of such a step but as a father he wanted to protect his daughter and as a monarch he wanted to secure the safety of someone who, though still technically heir presumptive, seemed now sure to inherit the throne. Elizabeth had her way: early in 1945 she joined the ATS, the Auxiliary Territorial Service, the women's army.

She did her training with No. 1 Mechanical Training Centre at Aldershot. The role yielded endless photo opportunities: whether fashion shots like those of Dorothy Wilding portraying the Princess elegant in officer's uniform or more prosaic studies in which Second Subaltern Windsor, clutching a spanner, is peering purposefully into the engine of some military vehicle. More importantly, it gave her a chance to consort with people far outside the royal circle and to discover that, in competition with other women of the same age, she was quite as quick to learn and rather more retentive in her memory than the majority of her contemporaries.

There was an element of make-believe about her training. Left to themselves, the authorities would have isolated her from the rank and file and confined her social life to the officers' mess; it took a resolute protest on her part to ensure that she was allowed to consort with the other recruits. However, she never succeeded in overcoming her father's insistence that each night she should return to sleep at Windsor. It was the nearest that Elizabeth was ever going to get, nonetheless, to doing the sort of work that was the lot of most of her future subjects. The confidence she gained from the experience was to serve her well in the years to come.

VE Day found her in London. Eight times the King and Queen with their two daughters appeared on the balcony of Buckingham Palace, eight times a huge crowd bellowed its ecstatic welcome. The princesses begged to be allowed to venture out into the streets; the King

hesitated, then finally gave way. 'Poor darlings,' he wrote that night in his diary, 'they have never had any fun yet.' Even in this moment of liberation they were escorted by Crawfie and a phalanx of courtiers and young army officers, but they had escaped the Palace walls, they were largely unrecognized, they were more nearly at one with the nation than they had ever been before. Elizabeth knew that liberty was a forbidden fruit and that this taste of it must be fleeting, but it was still a moment to be savoured.

Princess Elizabeth, Queen Elizabeth, Prime Minister Sir Winston Churchill, King George VI and Princess Margaret on the balcony of Buckingham Palace, VE Day, 8 May 1945.

She could never escape her royal destiny, but that destiny was about to be profoundly modified. In July 1939 the royal family had paid a visit to the Royal Naval College at Dartmouth. A young cadet, Prince Philip of Greece, met the two princesses and was later invited to tea on the royal yacht, *Victoria and Albert*. 'Philip came back aboard *V & A* and was a great success with the children,' wrote his uncle and the King's second cousin, Lord Mountbatten, in his diary. It is hard to believe that Mountbatten did not privately calculate that he might be introducing his nephew not just to his future Queen but to his future wife. Philip was obviously eligible. As a direct descendant of Queen Victoria he was related to Elizabeth, but not too closely. His father, Prince Andrew of Greece, was living in the South of France and Philip had only the most tenuous connection with what was theoretically his motherland: his education had been mainly British, his greatest ambition was to join the Royal Navy. He was five years older than the Princess, dashingly good looking and very obviously both forceful and intelligent.

The romantics insist that, from the time of this first meeting, Elizabeth never looked at another man. Certainly by the end of the war insider gossip frequently linked their names. The King at first resisted the idea, not because he disapproved of Philip but because his daughter was so young and he dreaded the disintegration of his close-knit family – the 'Family Firm' that had sustained him throughout the war. He fought a rearguard battle, but by the time the King and Queen, accompanied by the two princesses, left England on HMS *Vanguard* in February 1947 for a four-month visit to southern Africa, the belief was general that an engagement would soon be announced.

Elizabeth became twenty-one while in South Africa. On that day she broadcast to the Empire and Commonwealth. Her closing words were a resounding affirmation of her personal faith:

I declare before you all that my whole life, whether it be long or short, shall be devoted to your service and the service of our great imperial family to which we all belong. But I shall not have the strength to carry out this resolution alone unless you join in it with me, as I now invite you to do. I know that your support will be unfailingly given. God help me to make good my vow and God bless all of you who are willing to share in it.

No one who knew her doubted that she meant every word and would observe them faithfully throughout her life.

Her engagement to Philip Mountbatten – by now a British citizen and shortly to be transmogrified into the Duke of Edinburgh – was announced soon after the return from southern Africa. There were two schools of thought about the wedding. Some said that the marriage of the heir to the throne should be a grandiose as well as a joyous occasion: after the long years of war and painful recovery the nation deserved a dose of pageantry and conspicuous jollification. Others believed that, in a time of continued austerity, any ostentatious ceremony would be out of place. The Camden Town First Branch of the Amalgamated Society of Woodworkers sternly told the King 'that any banqueting and display of wealth will be an insult to the British people at the present time'. The spoilsports lost: the wedding was celebrated with conspicuous pomp and circumstance and though at first there was some grumbling, by the day itself the nation was united in an astonishing display of popular enthusiasm.

The royal marriage marked a significant change in the British people's perception of the royal family. The King was still most evidently there and as conscientious as ever in the execution of his duties, but he was no longer the sole, or even the principal, occupant of the limelight. He was now the past; Elizabeth was the future. He was known to be a dangerously sick man: nobody consciously looked forward to the ending of his reign, but there was a general acceptance that it could not be very long delayed. The intervening years were to be lived through with as little pain as could be managed; after that would come the dawning of a new age for Britain that would be altogether brighter and more glorious.

Every loving father feels a wrench when he hands his daughter over at the altar. That night George VI wrote to Elizabeth:

I was so proud of you ... on our long walk in Westminster Abbey, but when I handed your hand to the Archbishop I felt that I had lost something very precious ... I have watched you grow up all these years with pride ... and I can, I know, always count on you, and now Philip, to help us in our work. Your leaving us has left a great blank in our lives but do remember that your old home is still yours ... I can see that you are sublimely happy with Philip which is right but don't forget us is the wish of Your ever loving and devoted, Papa.

The plan had been that the newly married couple should install themselves in Sunninghill Park, a royal property in Windsor Great Park. Inconveniently, it burnt down before they could move in. Instead they rented a house in Surrey, Windlesham Moor, but it was intended only for weekend use and it never felt like home. In London, for almost a year, they moved into Princess Elizabeth's former apartments in Buckingham Palace. They were back in the 'old home' sooner than they had hoped. Even when the building is on such a massive scale, sharing accommodation with the bride's family is not the ideal start to married life. It was a relief when they could move into the heavily refurbished Clarence House a few hundred yards down the Mall. This was not until July 1949, however. By then Elizabeth had been for more than six months a mother.

For the first time in many generations the birth of a potential heir to the throne was not graced by the presence of the Home Secretary lurking in an anteroom. The King, always one for tradition, had wanted the custom to be maintained, but when the Commonwealth governments began to suggest that they too should be represented at the birth, it was realized that the whole thing could degenerate into a portentous farce and the idea was dropped. Other problems remained, however. Philip had taken the surname of his uncle and maternal grandfather, Mountbatten. Was the new Prince therefore Charles Mountbatten? The question was avoided – he was Prince Charles and that was enough – but the issue of what surname, if any, would be borne by the descendants of the future Queen and the Duke of Edinburgh was to remain a matter of contention for many years.

Philip was determined to keep his naval career going for as long as possible. In October 1949 he was posted as second-in-command of a destroyer with the Mediterranean Fleet. He was based in Malta. Until Prince Charles was born, Philip's wife was able only to spend a few months with him, living with his uncle, Lord Mountbatten, who had reverted from being a Supreme Commander and a Viceroy to become Commander of the First Cruiser Squadron of the Mediterranean Fleet. After Charles's birth, however, and for the next two years, she managed to spend most of her time as a naval officer's wife in Malta. No more than when she was serving in the ATS could her life be entirely normal. Though they established themselves in their own house – not much grander than those occupied by other naval officers of the same rank – Mountbatten continued to keep an avuncular eye on them and involved the Princess in more protocol-ridden occasions than she would have chosen for herself. But she was still able to drive her own car wherever she wanted, to drop in on a match of polo in which her husband was playing, to dine and dance at a local hotel, without noticeable escort or pestering by the press.

She cherished her freedom but knew that it could not last for long. Her father was every day becoming less able to carry the burden of the monarchy. He had smoked heavily for many years, his lungs had been badly affected and towards the end of 1948 early arteriosclerosis was diagnosed. At one time it seemed possible that he would lose a leg. A few months later major lung surgery proved necessary. Though it had not yet been detected, cancer was also latent. By the middle of 1951 it was obvious that he would never recover sufficiently to undertake all his royal duties. More and more his heir and daughter would have to share the burden. The Duke of Edinburgh realized that he would have to sacrifice his career to his wife's new role. Ever since he had married he had known that this would happen in the end; the end had come earlier than he had hoped but he accepted the inevitable with remarkably good grace.

By the time that a second child, Princess Anne, had been born, the ménage had re-established itself in Clarence House. Elizabeth's first private secretary, Jock Colville, had been replaced by a professional soldier, Martin Charteris. It was a change for the better. Colville was highly intelligent, sophisticated and diligent, but his outlook was conventional and his values were irredeemably those of the Establishment. Charteris was just as much a member of the Establishment but he had a genius for informality. He was totally loyal and devoted to his employer, but he was funny, irreverent and adept at knowing exactly how far he could go, usually going a little further, but never overstepping the outer reaches of propriety. He was to remain with Elizabeth for twenty-seven years. No man is indispensable, but her task would have been immeasurably more difficult without his presence.

One by one, Elizabeth took over the ceremonial duties that her father found too onerous. Most significant and most noticeable was Trooping the Colour, the annual birthday parade. The slight, trim figure in the scarlet tunic of the Grenadier Guards, surrounded by her loyal troops, was compared by innumerable sentimental commentators to her great ancestor, Queen Elizabeth I, addressing the troops at Tilbury as the Armada loomed threateningly in the Channel. The analogy was far-fetched but it was still a telling one. The Princess's presence on horseback among her troops caught the nation's imagination and reminded anyone who needed the reminder how close she was to the throne.

A visit to Canada had long been planned and in October 1951 she and the Duke set off on a tour that was extended to include a brief visit to the United States. It was in some ways a chastening experience. The Canadians remembered her endlessly smiling mother from the visit in 1939 and there was some criticism in the papers of the solemn, even surly expression that came over the Princess's face when in repose. Obviously, they surmised, she must be bored by what she saw. Martin Charteris pleaded with her to look more cheerful. 'My face is aching with smiling,' she retorted. Once the royal party got away from the cities of the east things began to go better and by the time that they moved on to Washington morale was high. They stayed with President Truman and their success was instant and emphatic. 'We've just had a visit from a lovely young lady and her personable husband,' Truman told George VI. 'They went to the hearts of all the citizens of the United States ... As one father to another we can be very proud of our daughters.' According to the *Washington Evening Star* he did not reserve his enthusiasm for his fellow father and head of state: 'When I was a little boy,' he said, 'I read about a fairy princess, and there she is.'

Even before the visit to Canada it had seemed likely that she would be called on to replace her father on a visit to Australia and New Zealand. Partly to gratify the inhabitants, more so as to provide a relatively tranquil break, the first step of the journey was to have been a stop-over of a few days in Kenya, which would have given the King a chance to watch some game and draw breath before the rigours that lay ahead. Princess Elizabeth was delighted to take on this undemanding duty. Accompanied by Winston Churchill, who had recently returned to power at the head of a Conservative government, the King on 31 January 1951 went to London airport to see his daughter off on what was to be a tour of several months. In theory he was on the road to recovery; in fact he looked alarmingly drawn and fragile. The goodbyes said, he returned to Sandringham. There, some time in the early hours of 6 February, he died in his sleep.

Elizabeth had spent a happy evening watching game at a waterhole: the exact time of her father's death could never be established, but she was probably up watching the sunrise at the time he died. Four hours after the body had been discovered the news filtered through to Sagana Lodge, the house given her by the Kenyan government to which she had returned after her game-watching the night before. Philip was told first and broke it as gently as he was able to his wife. To lose a much-loved father, even if one is to some extent prepared for it, is a painfully shocking experience; when the father is also the monarch and it is one's destiny to replace him the blow must be redoubled.

Once again, everything had changed. Her first thought was of the inconvenience that would be involved for other people. When her cousin Pamela Mountbatten, who was accompanying the party, went to her room to commiserate, the new Queen replied: 'Oh, thank you. But I am sorry that it means we've got to go back to England and it's upsetting everybody's plans.' But life had to go on. Martin Charteris asked her what she would wish to be called now that she had acceded to the throne. 'My own name, Elizabeth, of course,' she replied, 'what else?' It was the first significant decision that she made as Queen. In making it she showed the directness and common sense that was to be the hallmark of her reign.

Princess Elizabeth in January 1927 beside a photograph of her mother, who had just set off with the Duke of York on a six-month trip to New Zealand and Australia. Similar pictures were sent out to the Yorks at monthly intervals until their return in June. *Marcus Adams*

Princess Elizabeth, aged eight months, with her mother, the Duchess
of York, December 1926. The image was taken by Marcus Adams,
the son of another distinguished photographer, Walton Adams, who
had taken pictures of Queen Victoria.

OPPOSITE AND BELOW Princess Elizabeth in 1928, aged two. Marcus Adams, who specialized in photographing children, said that 'the delightful simplicity of a child calls for a simple pictorial statement'. But, 'Oh, the difficulty of portraying a child's expression.'

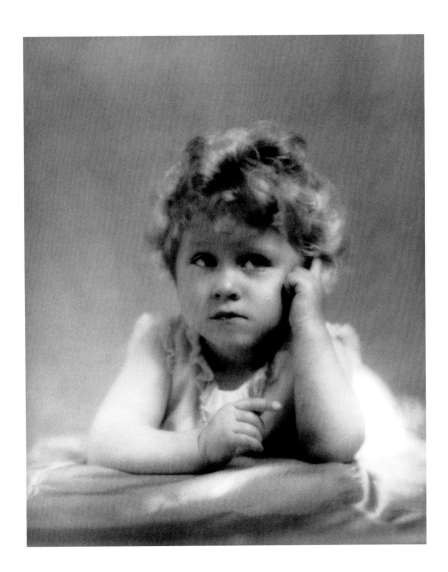

Princess Elizabeth with her sister, Margaret Rose, in August
1932 in the nursery at their maternal grandparents' home,
St Paul's Walden Bury in Hertfordshire. Horses, in all forms,
were a feature of the princesses' lives from an early age.

Princess Elizabeth pictured in November 1934 after acting as bridesmaid
at the marriage of her uncle the Duke of Kent and Princess Marina of Greece.
The photograph was taken by the Bassano studio, founded by Alexander
Bassano, one of the most successful of Victorian society photographers.

PREVIOUS PAGES, LEFT The Duke and Duchess of York
with the two princesses at Y Bwthyn Bach (The Little House)
in the grounds of Royal Lodge, Windsor, June 1936. The
miniature house was given to Princess Elizabeth by the
people of Wales in 1932. *Studio Lisa*

PREVIOUS PAGES, RIGHT Princess Elizabeth with her mother
and the corgis Dookie and Jane in the gardens behind their
home at 145 Piccadilly in July 1936. *Studio Lisa*

ABOVE AND OPPOSITE Two more studies by Marcus Adams.
The family group, photographed at Buckingham Palace in
December 1938, was reproduced extensively. The portrait
of Princess Elizabeth was taken in February 1939, two
months before her thirteenth birthday.

The self-taught portrait photographer Lisa Sheridan worked with her husband, James, under the professional name of Studio Lisa. In April 1940, nearly four years after her first visit to Royal Lodge, Windsor, she returned there to take more informal photographs of the royal family. The emphasis was on an unchanging family life just as the 'Phoney War' period was coming to an end. Later in the year some of these pictures were published in a book entitled *Our Princesses at Home* – to give succour to the troops and an idealized view of what they were fighting for.

ABOVE LEFT Princess Elizabeth with her mother, Queen Elizabeth. The two princesses lived at Royal Lodge for the first few months of 1940 and were reunited with their parents – occupied with morale-boosting visits around the country – at weekends. *Studio Lisa*

ABOVE RIGHT Princess Elizabeth with one of the royal corgis. Sheridan observed that: 'Princess Elizabeth still seems to me the more contemplative of the two sisters – the more reserved and the more sensitive.' *Studio Lisa*

LEFT The princesses picking daffodils in the grounds of Royal Lodge, Windsor, after one of their daily rides. The Royal Chapel of All Saints is in the background. *Studio Lisa*

Knitting for victory in 1940. According to Sheridan, 'when photographs are being taken the royal family enter wholeheartedly into the proceedings', including the King saying 'banteringly to Princess Margaret Rose: "Come on, now. Sit up for your picture!"' *Studio Lisa*

The two princesses at Windsor Castle in March 1941. When Hitler invaded the Low Countries in May 1940, Elizabeth and Margaret Rose moved from Royal Lodge into the more secure Castle – sleeping in the dungeons during air raids – and spent most of the rest of the war there. *Marcus Adams*

Queen Elizabeth with her two daughters in March 1941. A vision of domestic happiness was deemed an essential part of the war effort. *Marcus Adams*

Princess Elizabeth as a Sea Ranger and Princess Margaret Rose (as she would be known for a little longer) as a Girl Guide in 1943. Senior Guides were known as Rangers and those with a naval interest as Sea Rangers. Princess Elizabeth became one in February 1943 and this photograph was released for her seventeenth birthday in April that year. Dorothy Wilding, the well-known society photographer who took this picture, had been photographing members of the royal family since 1928 and in 1943 received a Royal Warrant.

Princess Elizabeth in October 1942, wearing the insignia of the Grenadier Guards, of which she had been made Colonel in February that year following the death of her godfather the Duke of Connaught, who had previously held the post. *Cecil Beaton*

ABOVE The two princesses at Buckingham Palace, October 1942. Cecil Beaton introduced a new mood of romanticism into portraits of the royal family and was one of the very few photographers who was invited to the Palace rather than applying for the right to a session.

OPPOSITE Princess Elizabeth in November 1943 at Windsor Castle: a photograph released the following year to mark her eighteenth birthday. *Cecil Beaton*

OPPOSITE In February 1945 Princess Elizabeth joined the Auxiliary
Territorial Service (ATS) as No. 230873 Second Subaltern Elizabeth
Alexandra Mary Windsor. In July, shortly before the end of the war,
she became a Junior Commander. *Dorothy Wilding*

ABOVE Princess Elizabeth in 1946, aged twenty. The Cartier bracelet
of diamonds and sapphires was an eighteenth-birthday present from
her parents. *Dorothy Wilding*

OPPOSITE AND BELOW Photographs from March 1945, which, in
their glamorous presentation and use of a dramatic background,
could only have been taken by Cecil Beaton. In the photograph
below Elizabeth is wearing one of her mother's altered pre-war
Norman Hartnell gowns. The photographs were not released
until February 1946, when the war was over.

The composed informality of Dorothy Wilding's family
group in the Music Room at Buckingham Palace in
May 1946 prefigures James Gunn's famous painting of
1950, *Conversation Piece at the Royal Lodge, Windsor*.

A photograph by Baron of Princess Elizabeth and the
newly created Duke of Edinburgh on their wedding day,
20 November 1947. Baron, whose real name was Sterling
Henry Nahum, was a friend of the Duke.

Princess Elizabeth's wedding dress was designed by Norman
Hartnell and was made from ivory satin embroidered with
ten thousand pearls imported from America. Hartnell, known
particularly for the embroidery on his gowns, designed many
dresses for the Queen over the next thirty years. *Baron*

OVERLEAF Bassano's formal wedding group. Queen Mary
and the Duke of Edinburgh's mother, Princess Alice of Greece,
are standing to the front on the left; King George VI, Queen
Elizabeth and Princess Alice, Countess of Athlone, are on
the right. The style of photograph – retouched to look like
a painting – was in vogue at that period.

Baron's christening portrait of Prince Charles with his mother,
Princess Elizabeth, 15 December 1948.

Cecil Beaton's touching vision of mother and child from December
1948, when Prince Charles was a month old. He observed later
how the Princess 'sat by the cot and, holding his hand, watched
his movements with curiosity, pride and amusement'.

Beaton, again indulging his fondness for dramatic backgrounds, took this photograph of Princess Elizabeth in December 1948. Beaton had earlier remarked how 'each time one sees her one is delighted to find how much more serene, magnetic, and at the same time meltingly sympathetic, she is than one had imagined'.

Princess Elizabeth at play with her infant son in her private sitting room at Buckingham Palace in 1949. With the deterioration in the King's health and his daughter's assumption of many of his duties, such relaxed time with her family was increasingly limited for the Princess. *Baron*

The proud parents, taken by Baron in 1949.

OPPOSITE AND ABOVE Two studies by Baron of Princess
Elizabeth at Clarence House, which became her home in 1949.
In the photograph above she is wearing the Girls of Great
Britain and Ireland tiara, which had been a wedding gift to
Queen Mary in 1893. It had been bought from money raised
by a committee chaired by Lady Eve Greville. Queen Mary
gave the tiara to Princess Elizabeth as a wedding present.

Baron's christening portrait: the infant Princess Anne in the
arms of her mother at Buckingham Palace, 21 October 1950.
Princess Anne wears the historic Honiton lace robe, which
had been worn by members of the royal family since 1841.

Prince Charles captures the attention of his mother and
grandmother at the christening of his sister, Princess Anne,
in 1950. *Baron*

BELOW AND OPPOSITE Princess Elizabeth with her daughter and in a family group in 1951. These were part of a portfolio of pictures taken at Clarence House by the Canadian photographer Karsh prior to the royal couple's first visit to Canada. Karsh arrived for the ninety-minute session with gifts of toys for the children; in return Prince Charles gave the photographer a daisy he had brought from the garden – he can be seen holding it in the picture. The background of the photograph has been heavily retouched.

OPPOSITE AND ABOVE Princess Elizabeth photographed
at Clarence House in July 1951. She reputedly described
these Karsh photographs as 'delicious'.

OPPOSITE AND BELOW Princess Elizabeth and the Duke of
Edinburgh at Clarence House in 1951. It was their London
home from 1949 to 1952. *Baron*

A black-and-white image of Princess Elizabeth and the Duke of Edinburgh from the 1951 photographic session with Baron.

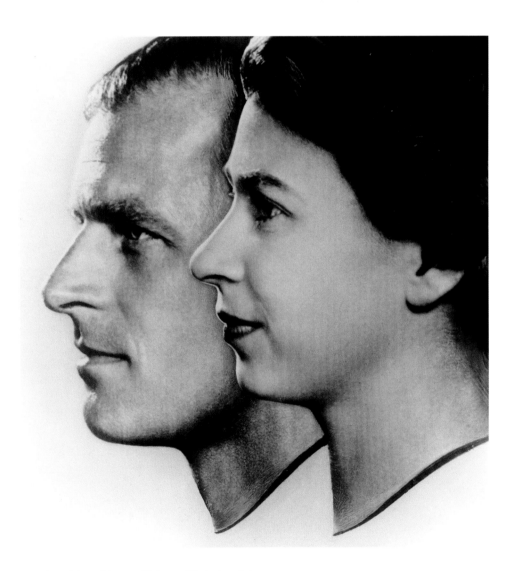

Karsh's celebrated image of Princess Elizabeth and the Duke of Edinburgh in profile. This montage was created from a photograph taken in 1951 although not released until the royal visit to Canada in 1957. The pose was replicated for the Golden Jubilee portfolio in 2002.

Princess Anne with her mother and Princess Margaret at Balmoral in 1951. *James Reid*

The royal couple in 1951. This was the year in which the Duke of Edinburgh gave up his active naval career in order to support Princess Elizabeth as she took on more of the routine tasks of monarchy from her ailing father. *Baron*

Princess Elizabeth, 1951. *Baron*

Dorothy Wilding's portraits of the Queen in 1952 show her
wearing a black taffeta strapless gown by Norman Hartnell.
The diamond necklace above was a twenty-first-birthday present
from the Union of South Africa and the diamond necklace in
the picture opposite was a wedding present from the Nizam
of Hyderabad.

In September 1952 Lisa Sheridan was again invited to take some photographs of the royal family, this time at Balmoral. Sheridan wanted a shot of the family on the steps of a sunken garden: 'The Queen called to Prince Charles and Princess Anne saying that she was the station master and that they should puff their trains once around the garden path before getting out on the platform beside her. In that way, the Queen helped me to make a peaceful camera calculation before the "trains" appeared on the scene again.' *Studio Lisa*

This was Sheridan's first encounter with the latest additions to the royal family: 'Prince Charles, though lacking nothing of Princess Anne's self-assured spirit, appears to be the more receptive and quietly thoughtful of the two.' *Studio Lisa*

II

THE NEW
ELIZABETHANS

1952–1976

The new Queen in May 1952 wearing the riband
and star of the Order of the Garter. She was appointed
a Lady of the Garter by King George VI in 1947,
when he presented her with the diamond-set Garter
star. It had been a gift to him from the Royal Navy
upon his marriage in 1923. *Dorothy Wilding*

The timing of Queen Elizabeth II's accession to the throne could, in one way, hardly have been more propitious, yet the factors that made it so were in the end to prove a considerable source of trouble. The dawn of the new reign was seen as a rebirth; the new Elizabethans would march united into a brave new world. 'Famous have been the reigns of our Queens,' intoned Churchill in a radio broadcast. 'Some of the greatest periods in our history have unfolded under their sceptre.' The monarchy, he maintained, was 'the magic link which unites our loosely bound but strongly interwoven Commonwealth'. Only gradually did it dawn on the British people that a new age had not dawned; Britain's place in the world remained very much what it had been before, unequivocally in the second rank behind the two superpowers and slipping inexorably downwards in terms of global influence. No one in their senses was going to blame the Queen for this but, just as she had been associated with exaggerated hopes, so she suffered when those hopes proved illusory. Her reign was to have been a period of triumph; instead it proved to be a long-drawn-out recessional: comfortable enough, prosperous even, but notably inglorious.

There were various immediate problems to be confronted. Clearly the new Queen was Elizabeth II of England, but what about Scotland, which had never known an Elizabeth I? James had been James I of England and VI of Scotland; surely the same should be true of Elizabeth? The Edinburgh Court of Sessions did not agree: the Queen was to be Elizabeth II both sides of the Tweed – a decision that affronted the growing forces of Scottish nationalism. And how was the ruling House to be styled? Was it now the House of Mountbatten, as Lord Mountbatten was rash enough to boast? The Duke of Edinburgh liked the idea, but would have been ready to settle for the House of Edinburgh. The Lord Chancellor would have none of it. George V, he claimed, had wanted the House to bear the name of Windsor so long as a direct heir was on the throne. 'Permanence and continuity', he argued, 'are valuable factors in the maintenance of a constitutional monarchy and the name of the royal family should not be changed if change can be avoided.' Philip complained that he was the only father in the land whose children did not bear his name: 'I'm nothing but a bloody amoeba,' he protested. It was another eight years before the Queen compromised by ruling that descendants who were not near enough to the throne to bear the title of His or Her Royal Highness should bear the surname of Mountbatten-Windsor.

Though she was not conscious of the fact, Elizabeth had been Queen from the moment of her father's death. There can be no interregnum in the British monarchy. The formal celebration of the new reign, however – delayed not merely by the wish to leave a decent interval in which the funeral baked meats could be removed but also by the enormously elaborate preparations which were called for – did not take place until 2 June 1953. The Coronation of Queen Elizabeth II was probably the most spectacular and, in the eyes of the participants at least, among the most memorable events of the twentieth century. As with any other great royal occasion, public attention was at first faltering and there was criticism of the antique and undemocratic flummery; then, as the day neared, criticism faded and public enthusiasm built up to a hysterical crescendo. As late as February 1953 less than half the population planned to watch or listen to the Coronation or mark the day in any other way. By May the proportion had risen to 70 per cent, and more than two million people – double the figure for George VI's Coronation in 1937 – were proposing to be on the route as the procession went by.

At first the interest was concentrated mainly in the south: it was a London affair, it was felt, only of faint interest in northern England, still less in Scotland or Wales. By June it had become a national affair: even the most distant hamlet found it necessary in some way to commemorate the day. It might have been expected that the more affluent and – with a small 'c' – conservative areas would show the more conspicuous enthusiasm. In fact it was in the slums or the near-slums that the show of flags and bunting was most unbridled; the more down-at-heel a London street, the more certain it seemed that it would rise joyfully to the occasion.

When the day came it was above all television that involved the nation in the celebrations. It was, of course, magnificent material for the cameras: yet it was not the pageantry and the flamboyance that struck a chord in the heart of the nation but the presence at the centre of it of a naturally shy and retiring woman, thrust by circumstances into the limelight. The film brought home, as no other rendering could have done, what the Coronation was all about. The Queen's pledges to her people; her patent sincerity and dedication; the burdens that, literally as well as metaphorically, were being heaped upon her: all struck the viewers with a freshness and immediacy that had been achieved, that could have been achieved, by no earlier Coronation ceremony.

Hundreds of thousands of people waving the Union Jack turned out to witness the Coronation of Queen Elizabeth II in Westminster Abbey on Tuesday, 2 June 1953. Many slept on the streets overnight in order to secure a good spot from which to see the procession.

It was touch and go whether the cameras would be allowed into Westminster Abbey. The Queen's initial feeling had been that the ceremony was already going to be a terrifying ordeal without the additional threat that some inadvertent gesture might be picked up and mar the whole effect. Eventually, her doubts were overcome. Television was still in its infancy. The number of licence holders doubled from 1.5 million to 3 million in the run-up to Coronation day; around every set clustered friends and neighbours – it was the most widely shared event in British history. The news that the New Zealander, Edmund Hillary, with the Nepalese Sherpa Tenzing Norgay, had scaled Everest, added a touch of the exotic to what was already one of the most memorable of days. 'The country and Commonwealth last Tuesday were not far from the Kingdom of Heaven,' rhapsodized the Archbishop of Canterbury.

The Coronation had emphasized the traditional nature of the royal family – yet those values were to be sharply questioned within a few months of its celebration. In 1953 the twenty-three-year-old Princess Margaret fell in love with the Comptroller of the Queen Mother's household, Group Captain Peter Townsend. Townsend was an outstandingly nice man whose charm and conscientiousness had endeared him to the King and Queen. He was a commoner, and thus outside the circles from which royal spouses were customarily drawn, but he had been a conspicuously gallant fighter pilot during the war and might well have been acceptable as a husband for the Princess if he had not been divorced and his wife still alive. Given the marital record of its founder, King Henry VIII, the Church of England's total rejection of divorce seems questionable, but it was nonetheless emphatic. Townsend was despatched to Brussels to serve as an air attaché at the British Embassy. It was hoped that absence would make the heart grow less fond and that the affair would not be revived once Townsend's posting was over.

It was revived, and in the autumn of 1955 the private problem became a public scandal. The people's opinion was divided, but a majority seems to have felt that love should be allowed to take its course. The Queen was torn between her desire for her sister's happiness and her obligation to follow the dictates of her ministers on any question of constitutional importance. So far as possible she refrained from expressing any opinion. The official view, however, was clear: if Margaret married Townsend she must sacrifice all the perquisites of royalty. The sacrifice proved too great, the affair was ended, but though the Queen was in no way to blame, a belief was fostered that the royal family was unduly blinkered and anchored in the past.

For Princess Margaret one benefit from this sad story was that it would be almost impossible for anyone to question her future choice of husband unless he suffered from the same disadvantage as Townsend. Five years later she became engaged to Antony Armstrong-Jones, a talented photographer. The fact that he was an Etonian and the stepson of an earl made him more or less acceptable to the upper classes; that he was, though partially disguised, a member of the vast and unaristocratic family of Joneses, gave him a certain status among those who wanted to see the Queen break out of her nineteenth-century cocoon. The marriage was a useful contribution to the campaign to democratize the royal family.

Such a campaign was becoming every day more necessary. In the autumn of 1957 the critics' attitude was voiced with unusual clarity. Lord Altrincham, editor of the *National and English Review*, devoted an issue to the monarchy. In his own article on the subject he criticized the Queen for bearing the debutante stamp: 'Crawfie, the London season, the racecourse, canasta and the occasional royal tour' would not have satisfied the first Elizabeth. The second Elizabeth surrounded herself with a tweedy and socially exclusive court and spoke in public with the style of 'a priggish schoolgirl, captain of the hockey team, a prefect, and a recent candidate for Confirmation'. Altrincham, or John Grigg as he once more became when he renounced the title, was personally one of the most temperate and generous of men, a monarchist who wished only to see the royal family move into the mid-twentieth century. This did not save him from being widely abused, slapped by an elderly member of the League of Empire Loyalists and challenged to a duel by an Italian monarchist. Yet the polls suggested that more than half the population felt that there was force in Altrincham's criticism.

Whether or not Altrincham's comments contributed to a feeling at court that something must be done to refurbish the royal image, it was about this time that some modest novelties were introduced. The snobbish ritual of presentation at court for debutantes was discontinued. Buckingham Palace was to some extent opened to the public by the conversion of the former chapel, ruined in the Blitz, into a gallery in which the royal art treasures could be exhibited. Informal parties were held at which trade unionists, headmasters and such unaristocratic worthies were entertained to lunch. Prince Charles was dispatched to a boarding preparatory school. The Queen's Christmas Day broadcast was for the first time televised. Things were palpably on the move.

The Queen was very conscious of the fact that not only was she Queen of Australia, Canada, New Zealand and a variety of other territories, but also Head of the Commonwealth. It was an institution that she took with great seriousness. The Commonwealth, in fact, could never have developed into the sort of superpower that was the aspiration of certain romantics and New Elizabethans. The Queen herself had no such exaggerated expectations, but she did believe that the Commonwealth had an important role to play in uniting the developed and the underdeveloped world and in fostering democracy and the rule of law as a prerequisite of membership. In November 1953 the Queen and the Duke of Edinburgh embarked on a gargantuan Commonwealth tour, primarily to accomplish the visit to Australia and New Zealand that had been aborted because of the King's death, but including ten days in Ceylon and brief calls in another dozen or so dependencies. It was on the final leg of this tour that the royal yacht *Britannia* was first used as a base for the royal tourists and a venue for gracious and grandiose entertaining. In time *Britannia* was to be much criticized as an example of ostentatious extravagance, but few lucky enough to experience it in its glory could doubt that it rendered fine service over many years.

The Queen was devoted to her first prime minister, but Winston Churchill was almost eighty years old by the time of the Coronation. No more than any of her ministers did she feel that it was good either for his reputation or for the future of the country for him to carry on. He clung to power, however, and if she ever hinted to him that it was time for him to go it must have been in tones so dulcet that he was able to ignore it. In June 1953, though, he suffered a severe stroke. With Anthony Eden, his obvious successor, undergoing a serious operation in an American hospital, it seemed that the Queen might soon have to make a difficult decision. In fact Churchill's condition remained a closely guarded secret, a small cabal of ministers and civil servants kept the show on the road, and Churchill largely recovered, but the incident had provided an alarming reminder that the royal prerogative could be more than a purely formal element of the constitution. Fortunately, by the time that Churchill finally accepted the inevitable and resigned, Eden was fully recovered. In theory the Queen could have sent for any other senior Conservative whom she felt might be able to command a majority in the House of Commons; in fact it was taken for granted by everyone, including Churchill, that Eden must be the next prime minister. Whether the Queen took any serious soundings is uncertain; if she did, it must have been in the knowledge that only one solution was possible. In April 1955 Eden took over at 10 Downing Street.

The Queen, on the six-month Commonwealth tour, 1953–54, accepts a bouquet from a Fijian girl at Suva, December 1953.

A little over a year later the Egyptian President, Colonel Nasser, nationalized the Suez Canal. Eden believed that he was confronted by a second Hitler and was resolved that there should not be another Munich. While publicly paying heed to the demands of the Labour Party and many of his own supporters that he should proceed against Egypt only through the United Nations, Eden covertly plotted with the French and Israeli governments and concocted a scenario by which the Israelis would attack Egypt and the French and British would intervene to separate the combatants and, incidentally, to reoccupy the Canal Zone. Mountbatten, now First Sea Lord, was foremost among those who told the Queen that this was militarily hazardous, morally indefensible and politically insane. She was in an impossible position. As Queen of the United Kingdom she could act only on the advice of her ministers; she could convey her private doubts to Eden but could not say anything publicly to dissociate herself from his actions. Yet as Head of the Commonwealth and Queen of many of its members, she knew that the great majority of the governments over which she presided were aghast and outraged by what was going on. That personally she shared this view seems certain; how much, if anything, she said to the Commonwealth prime ministers remains a matter for conjecture. Probably not much: in such circumstances the safest course must have been to listen to everyone and say as little as possible in reply.

The Suez debacle was followed almost immediately by the resignation, on the plea of ill health, of Anthony Eden. This time the situation was more complicated than it had been on Churchill's resignation, since there was no obvious successor. R.A. Butler and Harold Macmillan were the two main contestants. In terms of seniority 'Rab' Butler was the front-runner and almost all the press predicted that he would be chosen. Once he had ceased to be prime minister, Eden had no automatic right to advise the Queen, but it seems that he too favoured Butler and managed to make his views apparent. The Queen, however, believed that it was her duty to nominate the man who was the choice of the Conservative Party as a whole.

An element of mystery surrounds the proceedings, but two Tory grandees who were not themselves in contention, Lord Salisbury and the Lord Chancellor, Lord Kilmuir, were deputed to gather the views of the Cabinet. 'Is it Wab or Hawold?' Salisbury famously asked each member, and the answer from the great majority was that it was Hawold. The Chief Whip, Edward Heath, gathered the views of the Tory members of the House of Commons and reported that they, both as individuals and representing the feelings of their constituencies, also backed Macmillan. The Queen followed their advice. Opinions differ about the effectiveness of Macmillan's government, but she never had cause to fault him on his attitude towards the monarch. 'The Prime Minister is above all the Queen's first minister,' he once wrote. 'His supreme loyalty is to her.' Throughout his term of office he behaved as if that was literally the truth.

The Suez Crisis made it painfully obvious that the New Elizabethans were going nowhere: far from emulating their predecessors by venturing into new worlds, they were having the greatest difficulty in maintaining their position in the old one. The royal family, however, still enjoyed an almost sacrosanct status. However many people privately shared Lord Altrincham's doubts, remarkably little was said of it in public. When Prince Charles was sent to a boarding preparatory school and then on to Gordonstoun, the ruggedly horrific Scottish public school where his father had prospered and he suffered miserably, it was hailed as a miracle of progressive thinking. Some pointed out that it would have been more progressive still if the Prince had been educated at a state school, but the general view was that this was welcome evidence that the royal family was moving into the future. When Princess Anne followed in his footsteps by going to the elite girls' boarding school of Benenden, the process was seen to be irreversible.

It was almost a decade after Anne's birth that the Queen had returned from a tour of Canada to announce that she was once more pregnant. Princes Andrew and Edward were born in 1960 and 1964 respectively. There had been muttering among an ill-disposed minority that the royal marriage was, if not on the rocks, then at least in difficulties. The appearance of the two princes killed such rumours. The royal family was seen once more to exemplify familial stability, a shining example to the British people at a time when the divorce rate was soaring and the institution of marriage seemed under threat.

The Queen had to accept that the Empire which she had inherited from her father, already visibly crumbling at the time of her accession, was now in terminal disintegration. Her new prime minister was instrumental in accelerating that process. 'The wind of change is blowing through the Continent,' Macmillan had proclaimed on a visit to Cape Town, 'and, whether we like it or not, this growth of national consciousness is a political fact.' The Queen was resolved, however, that if she had anything to do with it, the end of Empire should only be a stepping stone in the growth of the Commonwealth. She devoted herself assiduously to cultivating the leaders of the new Commonwealth countries and to trying, by example if not by overt preaching, to show that there was much for everyone to gain from the development of close ties and mutual consultation.

A conspicuous example of this occurred in Ghana. In 1960 the Queen had been due to visit the newly independent country, but the visit had to be postponed because of the imminent birth of Prince Andrew. The Queen was anxious to repair the omission and was undeterred by the fact that Ghana had become a republic and that the new President, Kwame Nkrumah, was pursuing a markedly authoritarian policy and showing scant respect for the democratic values that were supposed to bind the Commonwealth together. When, shortly before the visit was due to start, a bomb exploded in the capital, Accra, Macmillan wondered whether he had not better advise the Queen to cancel her visit. She would not hear of it: if Ghana was wavering on the brink of anarchy or dictatorship, it was all the more important that she should try her hand as a moderating influence. Theoretically it was possible that if the British government had wished to stop her going she could have replied that she was not going to Ghana as Queen of the United Kingdom but as Head of the Commonwealth. In practice things could never have reached such a point, but if she had not insisted that it was not only her wish but also her duty to go, the visit might well have been abandoned. She went, and it was a great success. The Ghanaian government had been close to pulling out of the Commonwealth and throwing in its lot with the Soviet bloc: the Queen's visit did not transform Ghana into a pro-Western democracy, but it did help check a move towards the hard left which could only have taken place at the expense of the Commonwealth tie.

The Queen at Christiansborg Castle, Accra, with President Nkrumah of Ghana, during her 1961 State Visit to the country.

It was the same urge to promote the Commonwealth that led to Prince Charles, at the age of seventeen, being sent for six months to the Australian school of Timbertop. It was a step that he viewed with some apprehension, but after Gordonstoun almost anything was acceptable. He seems to have found the experience genuinely enjoyable. The pattern was followed for Princes Andrew and Edward, who spent time at schools in Canada and New Zealand respectively.

The transition from Churchill to Eden had been painless; from Eden to Macmillan had posed greater problems, but at least it had proved possible to establish beyond doubt the true wishes of the Conservative Party. In October 1963 it was another matter. Macmillan had intended to soldier on for at least a few more months; instead, on the eve of the Party Conference, he was struck down by a serious illness that called for a major operation. He resigned. Butler once more seemed the obvious successor, but Macmillan was resolved to thwart his ambitions. Lord Hailsham was second favourite, but he damaged his chances by a nakedly ambitious and mildly farcical performance at the Party Conference. The Queen visited Macmillan in hospital. As a resigning prime minister he had no right to advise her on his successor, but he contrived to make it clear that he favoured the Earl of Home. He claimed to have canvassed opinion widely throughout the party, but his consultations seem to have been limited and selective. Personally, the Queen must have been delighted. Home was a man whom she knew well, liked and trusted, and with whom she shared many common interests. She invited him to try to form a government.

A revolt ensued: Butler himself did not protest publicly, but the leading Tories Enoch Powell and Iain Macleod refused to serve under Lord Home. Ben Pimlott, the Queen's biographer, considered that this was 'the biggest political misjudgment of her reign'. She should have refrained from consulting Macmillan or, having done so, have rejected his advice. It seems, though, that if she had sought some other way of establishing the feeling of the Conservatives, the conclusion would have been much the same. A group within the party did feel that Home had been thrust on them without proper consultation but, in most cases, the objections were to the way the decision had been made, not to the end result. If this was really the Queen's 'biggest political misjudgment', it goes to show that her judgment was in general extraordinarily sound. One result of the imbroglio, however, was that the royal prerogative was further limited: the Conservatives resolved that its future leaders should be selected, not in hugger-mugger, but by secret ballot within the party.

Home did not last long and in October 1964 the Queen found herself confronted by her first Labour government. If she had any doubts about her relationship with a socialist prime minister, they must have been quickly dismissed. Wilson, already in awe of the monarchy as an institution, soon felt respect and affection for her as an individual. He attached great, some felt exaggerated, importance to his weekly audience, which grew longer and longer as his period in office wore on. He would come back in euphoric mood, and sometimes seemed noticeably to have modified his opinions as a result of what had been said. When he resigned she sent him a photograph of the pair of them in the rain at Balmoral, which he carried thereafter in his wallet.

Whatever the issue, Wilson was unequivocally on her side. When Tony Benn, then Postmaster-General, came up with a bright idea for a new set of postage stamps that would break with precedent by not featuring the monarch's head, he took them to the Palace and extolled their virtues. The Queen listened politely and, he thought, was well disposed towards the idea. In fact, she disliked it. Even as Benn was leaving the Palace she spoke to her private secretary. He got on to his opposite number at Number 10. The word was passed to Wilson. When Benn got back to his desk he found a message telling him to call the prime minister immediately. The new stamps were dead, he was told; his idea of omitting the royal head was never to be revived.

It was while Wilson was prime minister that the Queen found herself embroiled in a dispute in which she could not hope to play an unobtrusive role. In the autumn of 1965 Ian Smith, the premier of Southern Rhodesia, finally rejected constitutional changes that would have led, in the distant but not sufficiently distant future, to African majority rule. He made a Unilateral Declaration of Independence (UDI). This, he claimed, was compatible with loyalty to the monarchy; thus, in a bizarre adaptation of the rules of chess, seeking to use the Queen as a pawn in his designs. Wilson, for his part, saw the Queen as a vastly important ally in his efforts to bring the Southern Rhodesian government into line. His efforts foundered on the obdurate opposition of the Rhodesian hardliners, but the Queen proved more than ready to support his efforts, even to the extent of agreeing that Lord Mountbatten should fly out as her personal representative to confront the rebels. This project was, perhaps fortunately, aborted: it was to take another fifteen years of bloody attrition before the republic of Zimbabwe entered the Commonwealth.

Those in the Palace who were concerned with public relations, particularly the young and energetic Australian press secretary, William Heseltine, believed that the royal family was still dangerously remote from the British people. It was more than fifty years since the Keeper of the Privy Purse, Sir Frederick Ponsonby, had argued that: 'The monarchy must always retain an element of mystery. A prince should not show himself too much. The monarchy must remain on a pedestal.' Heseltine believed that it must get off that pedestal, or at least demonstrate that, however distinct its role might be, its members were still flesh and blood. His masterstroke was Richard Cawston's documentary film *Royal Family*, aired in June 1969. The camera was allowed to follow the Queen and her relations as they went about their duties or relaxed in private. They were portrayed as being hard-working, responsible and, above all, human. They are just like us, was the message of the film: their surroundings might be grander and their responsibilities more portentous, but what they really enjoyed was a picnic, a walk with their dogs, an evening in front of the telly. To an extraordinary extent the film changed the public perception of royalty. But this was achieved at a price. If the royal family could exploit its domestic life to improve its public image, it must also leave itself open to less sympathetic examination. The immunity that the royal family had enjoyed from intrusive scrutiny of its private life, already frayed, now virtually disappeared. This was to prove a damaging development when the royal children became old enough to commit serious indiscretions.

Princess Anne, the Queen, the Duke of Edinburgh and Prince Charles being filmed in 1968 for the BBC documentary *Royal Family*.

That the monarchy had another dimension, however, was illustrated vividly less than two weeks later when Prince Charles was invested Prince of Wales at Caernarfon Castle. Here the Queen and her family were displayed in quite another light. They were arrayed at their most splendiferous; performing arcane rituals that might seem faintly absurd but still demonstrated that there was something sublime and mysterious about the throne, a religious and spiritual element that transcended the conventional constitutional role to which the royal family was normally confined. What was more, the Investiture emphasized strongly something that the Queen had deeply at heart – that she was not Queen of England but of the United Kingdom.

Relatively few people questioned the expense of the Investiture, but the subject of money and the monarchy was becoming increasingly a matter for public concern. The problem was inflamed when the Duke of Edinburgh, on American television, declared that the finances of the royal family were on the point of going into the red. He had already, he said, been forced to sell his yacht and expected soon to have to give up polo. The sacrifices that he described and the place he chose to do it were perhaps ill-advised, but he had a point. If Britain wanted a royal family working more or less on the scale of the present one, it would have to pay for it. Harold Wilson managed to play the matter down, to adopt a bipartisan approach and refer the issue to a Select Committee, but the perceived extravagance of the royal lifestyle became a pet theme for republicans and other critics of the monarchy. It was to provide a potent element in the brew of discontent that was to mark the following decades of Elizabeth's reign.

By the time the Select Committee had reported, the Conservatives were back in power and Edward Heath was prime minister. Heath's most notable achievement – or worst crime, some would say – was to take Britain into Europe. His opponents advanced as one reason for their attitude the fact that British membership of the European Economic Community would diminish the standing of the monarchy. If the Queen had any qualms, she did not show them; what she must have deplored, however, was that Britain's entry into Europe inevitably

The Queen and Prince Charles at his investiture as Prince of Wales at Caernarfon Castle, 1 July 1969.

involved a weakening of the Commonwealth ties. Politically, the Commonwealth countries felt themselves distanced from Britain; economically – New Zealand in particular – they were disadvantaged. Somewhat grudgingly they accepted British entry; but if the Commonwealth had a coffin, another nail had been hammered in.

Heath was a man bereft of small talk and notoriously immune to female charms. It was said that the Queen, who had got on very well with Wilson, found him difficult to deal with. Almost certainly this is exaggerated: Heath himself frequently paid tribute to the value he attached to his relationship with the monarch. But his undisguised contempt for some of the more tempestuous Commonwealth governments, and his readiness to sacrifice their interests to his European dream, must have caused some concern at Buckingham Palace.

Even on board *Britannia*, there was business to be done. Here the Queen is going through her red boxes with her private secretary, Sir Martin Charteris, on a tour of islands in the Indian Ocean in March 1972. *Lichfield*

Heath lasted less than four years: early in 1974 Wilson was in office once again. His return to power illustrated how suddenly the monarchy might find itself called on to play a role of decisive constitutional importance. In the general election of February 1974 the Tories won marginally more votes than Labour but secured four fewer seats. Neither party had anything approaching an overall majority. The normal course would have been for Heath to resign and advise the Queen to send for Wilson, as leader of the largest party in the House of Commons. Instead, he hung on over the weekend following the election, trying to do a deal with the Liberals. Formally the Queen was not involved: Heath did not need to resign until he had been defeated in the House. In practice she must have been deeply concerned – the thing that she most wished to avoid was political instability and a botched-up coalition could only have led to this.

Nor did the problem end there. Heath failed in his efforts and resigned; Wilson formed a minority government. At any moment this might have been defeated. He would then have asked for a dissolution. Constitutionally the Queen was free to refuse the request and invite Heath or someone else to have another shot at putting together a stable coalition. Was this a practical possibility? Almost certainly she thought that it was not and would have given Wilson his dissolution even after a few weeks in office. In fact he held on for a respectable eight months before resigning. But it was another reminder of the fact that the royal prerogative was still a reality; that the Queen was not merely an ornamental figure, a symbol of national unity, but had a significant, even crucial, role to play in the working of the constitution.

Dorothy Wilding was invited to take the official portraits
on the Queen's accession to the throne in 1952. Many
of her photographs were subsequently used as the basis
for the new currency as well as for stamps in the UK
and Commonwealth.

Queen Elizabeth II and the Duke of Edinburgh
photographed by Baron on the circular landing above
the Grand Staircase at Buckingham Palace in 1953.

The Queen and the Duke of Edinburgh dressed for
the first State Opening of Parliament of the new reign,
November 1952.

ABOVE AND OPPOSITE The Queen wearing the star, riband
and badge of the Order of the Garter, 1953. The monarch
is sovereign of the Order of the Garter, which was founded
in 1348 and is the most senior of the British orders of
chivalry. *Baron*

The Queen wearing her Coronation robes, 2 June 1953, photographed at Buckingham Palace by Cecil Beaton against a backdrop of the Henry VII chapel at Westminster Abbey. 'The Queen looked very small under her robes and crown, her nose and hands rather pink – also her eyes somewhat tired. Yes in reply to my question, the crown does get rather heavy. One couldn't imagine that she had been wearing it now for nearly three hours.'

Queen Elizabeth II with her six Maids of Honour
at Buckingham Palace after the Coronation. *Cecil Beaton*

The Queen and the Duke of Edinburgh after the Coronation,
2 June 1953, in front of a backdrop of Westminster Abbey.
The Queen's dress, designed by Norman Hartnell, was
embroidered with flowers symbolizing Great Britain and the
Commonwealth. The Duke's uniform is that of an Admiral
of the Fleet. *Cecil Beaton*

The newly crowned Queen wearing the Imperial State
Crown and carrying the Orb and Sceptre. *Cecil Beaton*

ABOVE AND OPPOSITE The Queen pictured in 1953, on the small staircase of the Grand Entrance of Buckingham Palace, wearing a yellow tulle evening gown decorated with sprays of wattle, the national flower of Australia. She was about to embark on a lengthy Commonwealth tour that included two months in Australia; the photographs were scheduled for release to the press just before her arrival there. *Baron*

One of Beaton's most romantic studies of the Queen,
taken in 1955, wearing the insignia and mantle of the
Order of the Garter and seated before a backdrop of
St George's Chapel, Windsor, where the annual Garter
service is held each June.

Cecil Beaton photographing the Queen in November 1955
in the Blue Drawing Room at Buckingham Palace. 'There was
an ugly foggy pall coming into the Palace rooms ... Grim with
determination I conducted the Queen to the centre of a circle
of blinding lights ... No time for self-pity. I must go to do battle
as quickly as possible.'

'The Queen stood looking very inanimate and it was for me
now to keep her alert and amused – Luckily it seems that the
royal family have only to get a glimpse of me for them to be
convulsed with giggles.' *Cecil Beaton*

The Queen enthroned. Beaton recalled that Martin Charteris, the Queen's assistant private secretary, thought the Queen would be too self-conscious about sitting on the throne, to which the photographer responded: 'If she can't sit in that throne who can?' The picture was taken for the Queen's three-week tour of Nigeria in January–February 1956.

The Queen wearing a dress designed by Norman Hartnell, Grand Duchess Vladimir's tiara (set with emeralds), Queen Mary's Delhi Durbar necklace, the Dorset Bow brooch and the star, riband and badge of the Order of the Garter. The photograph was released just prior to a State Visit to France in April 1957. *Baron*

OVERLEAF Antony Armstrong-Jones, later Lord Snowdon, at one time an assistant to Baron, took these photographs of the Queen and the Duke of Edinburgh at Buckingham Palace in July 1957. He married Princess Margaret three years later and continued to take royal photographs even after their marriage had ended in divorce.

Another portrait by Snowdon of the Queen and the Duke of
Edinburgh at Buckingham Palace in 1957. These were all taken
for a visit to Canada in October that year. *Snowdon*

The Queen in 1957 wearing the Diamond Diadem made in 1820
for the coronation of George IV. Set with 1,333 diamonds, the
design features roses, thistles and shamrocks, the national emblems
of England, Scotland and Ireland. *Snowdon*

The royal family at Buckingham Palace in 1957. The piano
was more than a prop; the Queen was brought up to play
the instrument. Prince Charles, in a departure from royal
custom, started at a pre-preparatory school, Hill House,
in November 1956. Under the heading 'Singing', his first
report said that he had 'a sweet voice, especially in the
lower register'. *Snowdon*

The Queen at Sandringham, poised to make her
first live Christmas broadcast on television, 1957.

Princess Anne's seventh-birthday photograph, taken by
Snowdon during the same twenty-minute session in the
grounds of Buckingham Palace as the picture below, 1957.

One of Snowdon's most celebrated family groups, based on eighteenth-century
romantic paintings and taken in the grounds of Buckingham Palace in 1957.
The photographer had procured a rod and two trout so that the children could
be captured fishing. Unfortunately his housekeeper misread his intentions and
grilled the fish for his breakfast. They had to make do with a book instead.

OPPOSITE AND ABOVE Snowdon and Donald McKague discover the charms of
a balcony scene – on the circular landing above the Grand Staircase at Buckingham
Palace in 1958. In Snowdon's picture the royal couple are dressed for the State Opening
of Parliament – the first to be televised. In Donald McKague's photograph the Queen
is wearing a satin dress designed by Norman Hartnell and the Duke is in the uniform
of Colonel-in-Chief of the Royal Canadian Regiment – one of a series of images taken
for a six-week tour of Canada that the royal couple undertook in the summer of 1959.

The Queen and Princess Anne at Windsor, May 1959. From a young age the Princess was passionate about horses and riding. In 1971 she won the individual European Three-Day Event at Burghley and competed in the 1976 Montreal Olympic Games as a member of the British Three-Day Event team. *Studio Lisa*

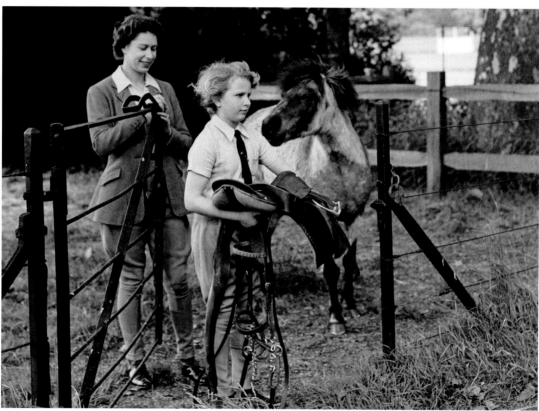

ABOVE AND OPPOSITE The Queen is wearing a day dress by Hardy Amies, who first designed outfits for her in 1951 and was the royal dressmaker until his retirement in 1990.

In order to bring the Queen nearer to the height of the Duke of Edinburgh for
these back-to-back profiles, the photographer Donald McKague asked the Queen
to stand on a low platform. Nonetheless, the respective height levels were not right
– until the Queen volunteered to remove her shoes. The finished photographs are
an unusual representation of a singularly united marriage.

OPPOSITE AND ABOVE The lake at Frogmore in Windsor Home Park
provided a suitable background in May 1959 for a mother and
daughter with a shared fondness for outdoor pursuits. *Studio Lisa*

1952–1976 137

The royal photographer is photographed – the wedding of
Princess Margaret and Antony Armstrong-Jones, 6 May 1960.
As well as the bride's sister, brother-in-law and mother, the
group includes Sir Robert Armstrong-Jones and the Countess
of Rosse, the groom's parents. Prince Charles was a page and
Princess Anne (seated third from the right) was a bridesmaid.
Cecil Beaton

ABOVE AND OPPOSITE Queen Elizabeth with her corgis
at Windsor Castle, 1962. Lisa Sheridan was now in
her third decade of taking royal portraits and received
a Royal Warrant from the Queen in 1964. *Studio Lisa*

The Queen with Prince Andrew at Windsor Castle, 1962.
Studio Lisa

The Queen first rode a horse when she was three and was given her first pony by George V at the age of four. The equestrian training continued at Windsor during the war and included learning how to handle a pony cart. Here she gives Prince Andrew some early instruction. *Studio Lisa*

The Queen in the grounds of Balmoral in 1964. Prince
Andrew is riding his pony, Valkyrie, and her nephew,
Lord Linley, leads the procession on his tricycle.
Godfrey Argent

The Queen with one of her favourite horses, Betsy,
photographed at Sandringham in 1964 by Godfrey Argent
who, as a former corporal of horse in the Household
Cavalry, was particularly well qualified to portray the
equestrian side of royal life.

Prince Edward was born in March 1964 and photographed by Beaton two months later. 'From the moment the family group assembled themselves in our white oasis in front of the camera the pattern seemed to form and the lighting proved as luminous as we had hoped. Moreover the infant showed bonhomie and an interest in the activity that was going on.'

ABOVE AND OPPOSITE The Queen at Windsor with her two
younger sons, Prince Andrew and Prince Edward, and one
of her dogs, 1965. *Studio Lisa*

The Queen relaxing at Windsor. She once told her riding instructor that if she had not been Queen she would have liked 'to be a lady living in the country with lots of horses and dogs'. *Studio Lisa*

OPPOSITE AND ABOVE In 1966 Karsh was invited back to take photographs of the Queen and the Duke of Edinburgh for Canada's centennial the following year. The Queen is wearing Queen Alexandra's Kokoshnik tiara. The picture opposite was taken in the White Drawing Room at Buckingham Palace.

The Queen at Buckingham Palace in 1968. 'I asked the
Queen to let me take some pictures in the mauve dress she
wore ... I felt the streak of sun coming through the Blue
Drawing Room onto the blue sofas would make a very
happy colour combination.' *Cecil Beaton*

OPPOSITE AND BELOW Beaton again, from his last session
with the Queen in October 1968. The photographs were
to be released to mark her forty-third birthday. The dress
had been designed by Hardy Amies for the State Visit to
Germany in 1965.

BELOW The Queen in 1968, wearing an admiral's cloak, stands in front of *The Review of the Fleet at Portsmouth by King George III* by Dominic Serres. *Cecil Beaton*

OPPOSITE This Beaton photograph of the Queen in the admiral's cloak is curiously reminiscent of the iconic 1954 Annigoni painting. He had difficulties with the pose until '*suddenly* she turned to the L. and the head tilted – and this was the clue to the whole sitting – the Tilt'.

OVERLEAF, LEFT Lord Lichfield, who, as a cousin of the Queen, shared with Lord Snowdon the privilege of being an insider as well as a professional photographer, took this picture of the Queen leaving Buckingham Palace in the Irish State Coach on her way to the State Opening of Parliament in 1971.

OVERLEAF, RIGHT The Queen in the mantle of the Order of the Garter, 1968. *Cecil Beaton*

Lord Lichfield's photograph of the royal family at Windsor in December 1971 was taken for the Queen and the Duke of Edinburgh's silver wedding celebrations in 1972. Seated, from left to right, Princess Margaret, the Duchess of Kent (with Lord Nicholas Windsor on her lap), Queen Elizabeth the Queen Mother, the Queen, Princess Anne, Marina Ogilvy and Princess Alexandra. Standing, from left to right, Lord Snowdon, the Duke of Kent, Prince Michael of Kent, the Duke of Edinburgh, the Earl of St Andrews, Prince Charles, Prince Andrew, Sir Angus Ogilvy and James Ogilvy. Seated on the floor, from left to right, Lady Sarah Armstrong-Jones, Lord Linley, Prince Edward and Lady Helen Windsor.

The Queen at the Ghillies' Ball, Balmoral, dancing the Dashing White Sergeant with a member of a highland regiment stationed at the Castle. She was photographed by Lord Lichfield, who was invited to Balmoral to take photographs for the silver wedding anniversary.

The Queen taking part in an eightsome reel at the Ghillies' Ball surrounded by other members of the royal family. *Lichfield*

The Queen enjoying an off-duty moment on the royal yacht
Britannia in the Indian Ocean, March 1972. Lord Lichfield,
fortunately armed with a waterproof camera, captured her laughing
at him being ducked as part of the crossing the line ceremony.

On tour aboard the royal yacht *Britannia* in 1972. The Queen
said that it was the one place she could truly relax. *Lichfield*

The royal family on holiday at Balmoral, photographed in
the late afternoon after a day's shooting. In these silver wedding
anniversary pictures Lord Lichfield was deliberately trying to
create a more informal image than the pictures taken of the
family at Balmoral in the 1950s and 1960s.

The Queen and the Duke of Edinburgh at Balmoral. Lord Lichfield worked hard to master the technique of backlighting. In order to take this photograph, he had to kneel uncomfortably on the grass beside a loch.

OPPOSITE The Queen herself suggested this
location on the burn called Garbh Allt on
the Balmoral estate. As soon as she sat down,
one of the corgis jumped onto her lap
and the photograph was made. *Lichfield*

The Queen at Balmoral doing what she most enjoyed.
The Castle has been in the personal possession of
the royal family since Queen Victoria's reign and the
Queen was said to feel more at home there than at
any other of the royal residences – it is where she spent
her summer holidays as a child. Here she points out
a cairn to the photographer. *Lichfield*

OVERLEAF Dinner aboard *Britannia* in 1972.
Lord Lichfield recalled that 'whenever possible,
I tried to catch the Queen and her entourage
in natural light and, after a few days, the click
of my shutter became just another element in
Britannia's smoothly running routine'.

OPPOSITE AND BELOW Two pictures taken at Windsor Castle
in 1975 by Peter Grugeon. Grugeon was a former civil servant
who opened a photographic studio in Reading and was startled
to be summoned, out of the blue, to take the photographs
that were released for the Queen's fiftieth birthday.

The Queen in the garden of Buckingham Palace, 1976, taken
for an article in the *Radio Times* about royal gardens. The
photographer Dmitri Kasterine recalled that: 'The Queen appeared
out of a door at the side of the Palace, alone except for her corgis,
and was instantly recognizable as an old friend. (After all, you had
known her all your life, even though you had never met her.) She
walked directly towards us, smiled and asked me where I wanted
her to stand. I made doubly sure the camera was set correctly and
took the pictures. There seemed to be no hurry – the dogs needed
walking after all.'

The Queen at Lord Lichfield's wedding reception, Eaton
Hall, Cheshire, 1975. In the centre is Princess Margaret
with a young Lord Linley. Dmitri Kasterine, who took
this picture, had been the first photographer to employ
Lord Lichfield fulltime.

III

THE MIDDLE YEARS

1977–1996

The Queen at Government House, Wellington, taken by
the New Zealand photographer Ronald Woolf after the State
Opening of the New Zealand Parliament in 1986. She is
wearing the Sovereign's Badge of The Queen's Service Order
of New Zealand with the Garter riband and star.

The British people like their monarchs to be very young or very old: Queen Elizabeth II confronting a new dawn for her country or Queen Victoria, the Widow of Windsor, a dumpy figure in mourning black, cooped up in her castle, mistress of a vast empire, mother and grandmother of Europe's royalty, immeasurably the most important woman in the world. By the middle of the 1980s the Queen was neither of those things. 'My mother is a star, my daughter-in-law is a star, where does that leave me?' she is said once ruefully to have enquired.

The last quarter of the twentieth century was to be uniquely testing so far as the monarchy, indeed the Queen herself, was concerned. Almost before it had begun, however, both in the shape of an individual and as an institution, the Crown received an unexpectedly positive reaffirmation of its place in the nation's affections.

The Silver Jubilee, marking the twenty-fifth anniversary of the Queen's accession, took place in 1977. The circumstances did not seem propitious for any kind of celebration. The country could hardly have been in more dire financial straits. Inflation was running at a catastrophic 16 per cent: it was only a few years since Lord Rothschild had pronounced that any country whose inflation exceeded 10 per cent qualified as a banana republic. There were more than a million and a half unemployed. The Chancellor of the Exchequer had been forced to go with begging bowl to the International Monetary Fund to seek a huge loan. Every kind of public expenditure was being scrutinized with a view to possible economies. It was hardly the moment to indulge in conspicuous expense on lavish parades or other festivities. The Queen herself was very doubtful whether her people could be in the mood to join in any form of rejoicing. At the end of 1976 there seemed every reason to believe that her doubts were justified.

At that date only a handful of people had even taken in the fact that there was to be a Jubilee the following year. There did not seem to be anything much to celebrate. Even if it was felt that the passage of twenty-five years was something remarkable, the twenty-five years in question were surely a cause for lamentation rather than rejoicing. They had witnessed a decline in Britain's standing as a world power that can rarely have been matched in national history. Nobody supposed that this was in any way the Queen's fault, but just as her renown would have been enhanced by a period of glory, so it was diminished by association with failure. Not only was there nothing to celebrate, there was not even anything to get excited about. The Jubilee would be a non-event. Nobody cared.

Slowly at first and then at an ever more hectic pace, the national mood changed. There had been pockets of enthusiasm from the start. The Jubilee was formally to be celebrated in June, but on the day of the actual accession, in cold and pouring rain on a miserable February night, the villagers of Shilton in Oxfordshire gathered at the church, sang an anthem and then processed to the village pond where they sang 'Land of Hope and Glory'. By the time the country had emerged from a singularly bleak and joyless winter the feeling was growing that the inhabitants of Shilton were not just cranky eccentrics, to be viewed with derision, but might, after all, have got a point. Perhaps it really was time for a party. Once the idea took root it spread extravagantly. The very fact that there was no strong encouragement from on high seemed to inspire each street and village to undertake its own private celebration. Decorations began to proliferate; al fresco parties were organized in what might have seemed the most unpromising locales. The exuberance of the royalist rally was indeed so marked that not even the most determined anti-monarchist could ignore it. All over Britain a frenzy of last-minute preparation took place as communities which, through disapproval or inattention, had neglected to provide any kind of local revelry, belatedly decided that something must be done after all.

The intention had been to keep the festivities resolutely low-key: if the public chose to make a party of it, then well and good; if not, then at least it could not be said that the hopes of the courtiers had been disappointed. The heart of the celebration, a procession to St Paul's followed by a Thanksgiving Service, though spectacular enough, was not intended to rival the Coronation. There were no stands along the route and few decorations. Nobody knew whether huge or even respectably large crowds would be attracted. By the evening before, the doubts of the sceptics were being silenced; by nine on the following morning people were already five or six deep the whole way along the route and more were pouring in from every direction. A million people watched the Golden Coach take the Queen and Prince Philip from the Palace to St Paul's. Behind them rode the Prince of Wales in the scarlet uniform of a Colonel of the Welsh Guards. In the speech at Guildhall that followed the service the Queen renewed the promise that she had made in South Africa thirty years before. 'When I was twenty-one,' she said, 'I pledged my life to the service of our people and I asked for God's help to make good that vow. Although that vow was made in my salad days, when I was green in judgment, I do not regret or retract one word of it.' No more in 1977 than in 1947 could anyone have doubted her absolute sincerity.

The mood in the provinces seemed little different from that in London. Everywhere the Queen went within the British Isles she was rapturously received. There were doubts as to whether it was wise to include the scheduled visit to Northern Ireland. The Home Office advised that there were bound to be serious risks and urged her to stay at home. Her private secretary asked her whether she wished to go ahead with the plans. 'Since we've *said* I'm going,' she observed, 'I want you to say that I'm going.' She went.

The Jubilee was remarkable for what it did not show. There seemed to be so many reasons to expect that things had changed, that people had ceased to feel any real interest in the monarchy, that the national fervour whipped up by the Coronation could never be revived. Yet, after the initial apathy and the routine complaints about expense and wasted effort, all had gone as not even the most enthusiastic royalist could have believed possible. Everything had changed, yet nothing, it seemed, had changed.

***

By the time of the Jubilee, Margaret Thatcher had for two years been leader of the Conservative Party. Her assertive personality had already made a strong impression on the British people. When the VIPs were beginning to make their way up the steps of St Paul's for the Jubilee service, a girl in the crowd speculated on the whereabouts of Mrs Thatcher: 'She'll arrive in the Golden Coach instead of the Queen, you'll see!' Jokes suggesting that the Leader of the Opposition thought herself as much a monarch as a future prime minister were often heard.

In 1979 she duly began her reign in 10 Downing Street. As a woman of more or less the same age, bearing heavy responsibilities and painfully aware that she was perpetually in the public eye, the Queen might have been expected to greet her new prime minister with enthusiasm. Perhaps she did; even more than earlier monarchs, the Queen was consummately skilful at concealing her true feelings about the political figures with whom she had to deal. The public perception, however, was that the Queen took little pleasure in Mrs Thatcher's company and felt some resentment at her propensity to hog the limelight at moments when the monarch might have been expected to play the leading role.

If this were so, it certainly did not stem from any lack of respect on Mrs Thatcher's part for the institution of monarchy. She was, indeed, almost excessively reverential and in public at least displayed a marked respect for the Head of State. But there are many reports that point to a lack of rapport, an impression that the two did not enjoy each other's company, that their conversations were at the best stilted, sometimes downright uneasy. 'These were two women who registered different vibrations,' Hugo Young, a biographer of Mrs Thatcher, observed. Nobody except the two women involved could know how marked this was in the weekly audiences in Buckingham Palace, but it was painfully apparent during the annual pilgrimage to Balmoral that every prime minister is required to undertake. Mrs Thatcher was an urban animal to her fingertips; she could not see the point of country sports or midge-plagued picnics on barren hillsides. She was ill at ease and made little effort to suggest the contrary.

The common complaint of the less discreet courtiers was that Mrs Thatcher was more regal than the Queen. She adopted the royal 'we' with embarrassing ease, and when the country went to war to liberate the Falkland Islands from the Argentinians in 1982 she took the salute at the victory parade in the City of London. This was a role that many people felt would better have been played by the Queen, especially since Prince Andrew (always alleged to be her favourite among the royal children) had served as a helicopter pilot in the campaign and had been exposed to considerable danger.

What was more significant than any such personal differences was the very real political and ideological divide between the monarch and the prime minister. Most conspicuously this related to the Commonwealth. Like Ted Heath before her, Mrs Thatcher considered the Commonwealth to be an irritating nuisance and the Commonwealth Conferences, at which Britain usually found itself assailed from all sides for its policies in southern Africa, at the best a waste of time and at the worst a damaging opportunity for developing nations to attack the values and policies of the West. As Head of the Commonwealth and Head of State of many of its members, the Queen had some sympathy with the criticisms of the British government and, anyway, felt that it was better that the disagreements should be aired and the complaints of developing nations listened to with attention.

Sonny Ramphal, Secretary General of the Commonwealth and a man viewed with considerable suspicion by Mrs Thatcher, told Ben Pimlott: 'First the Queen brought an understanding that it was a post-colonial Commonwealth, something even senior members of the Foreign Office didn't understand. Second, she brought a new quality of caring, a sense that it was an important dimension of her reign, and not just tacked on to being Queen of England. Her success in Commonwealth countries has derived from an awareness that she cared.' The Queen established excellent personal relations with the more tempestuous Commonwealth leaders, such as Kenneth Kaunda, Julius Nyerere or Lee Kuan Yew. One knows as little about what she actually said to them in her private conversations as one does about her audiences with her British prime ministers. It is unlikely that she ever committed herself to any point of view which she knew to be directly contrary to the views of the British government; it would be equally surprising, however, if she had not given the impression that she was listening sympathetically and that she understood the reasons for their attitudes.

It was at the Commonwealth Conference in Zambia in August 1979 that her influence was most notably to be observed. Mrs Thatcher had at first intended to give the conference a miss and, on grounds of security, suggested that it would be wise for the Queen also to stay away. If this had been translated into firm advice the Queen would probably regretfully have accepted it, but the government wisely left the final decision to the Queen. She had no hesitation. 'It is the firm intention', announced Buckingham Palace, 'that the Queen will be going.'

Probably the Queen's decision was a factor in Mrs Thatcher's change of heart. She went to Lusaka expecting fierce criticism of British inaction over Southern Rhodesia, to find that, in part at least because of the emollient efforts of the Queen, the atmosphere was far more positive than she had expected. Constructive talks took place and more common ground was established than had seemed possible before the conference. Four months later the Lancaster House Agreement ended the civil war and set up the new state of Zimbabwe. The agonies that that country has subsequently endured should not lead one to forget how dire the situation in Southern Rhodesia had previously been and how bright the prospects for the new country had seemed in the first few years of independence.

But there were even more fundamental differences of view that divided prime minister and monarch. Whatever government might be in power, the Queen was a consensualist, always anxious to avoid stark confrontations, with all the tension and social unrest that such policies involved. Mrs Thatcher believed confrontation to be necessary if not desirable: if social unrest was the price, it was one worth paying in the interests of putting Britain back on the path to prosperity. 'There is no such thing as society,' Mrs Thatcher famously declared; nothing is more important than society, the Queen would have countered. One did not need to be a particularly acute or well-informed observer to see that such widely differing attitudes would be bound, from time to time, to create tension between the Palace and Number 10.

Nobody was prepared, however, for the article in the *Sunday Times* on 20 July 1986, when the political editor, claiming to base his story on 'sources close to the Queen', described the royal consternation at the policies pursued by Mrs Thatcher's government. The Queen, it was claimed, felt her prime minister to be 'uncaring, confrontational and socially divisive'. The government was indifferent to the needs of the poor, wilfully aggressive in its approach to the unions, unwise in the support it had given to the recent American air attacks on Libya. No individual was credited with this interpretation of the royal views, but the rest of the media quickly concluded that only Michael Shea, the Queen's press secretary, could have been responsible. Nobody suggested that the Queen herself had specifically authorized his utterances, but there was plenty of speculation that he would hardly have dared to speak so unequivocally if he had not felt confident of his employer's approval.

The Queen's private secretary, now Sir William Heseltine, was quick to contradict such allegations. In a letter to *The Times* he claimed that, while the Queen was constitutionally entitled to have opinions of her own on government policy and to express them to her chief ministers, she regarded such intercourse as entirely confidential. It was 'preposterous' to suggest that she would seek publicity for her views. Shea had indeed spoken on several occasions to the political editor of the *Sunday Times* but nothing he had said could reasonably bear the interpretation put upon it by the article. To maintain the contrary constituted 'a totally unjustified slur on the impartiality and discretion of senior members of the Royal Household'. Shea himself claimed that the article had made bricks with a minimal amount of straw. Was the Queen unhappy about the coal strike? he had been asked. 'The Queen is always unhappy when the country is in turmoil,' had been his reply. 'The Queen is deeply disturbed by the government's treatment of the miners,' had been the *Sunday Times*'s interpretation of his words. The impression left in the mind of the public – probably well justified – was that the Queen had neither authorized nor welcomed the article, but that it had given a pretty accurate picture of what she really felt.

***

In August 1979 the Queen had been brutally reminded of the perils to which all those in the public eye are subject when Prince Philip's uncle, Lord Mountbatten, the former Viceroy of India and Chief of the Defence Staff, had been murdered by the IRA while in his boat off the west coast of Ireland. Mountbatten had never played quite as significant a role in the counsels of the royal family as he liked to imagine, but he was well liked, trusted, and one of the few people with whom the Queen could talk in terms of informal intimacy. With Martin Charteris having retired two years before and the Queen's closest friend among the courtiers, Lord Plunket, having died in 1975, there were sad gaps among the old familiar faces that had made Buckingham Palace more than just an austere place of work. Mountbatten was doubly missed since he was one of the few people who could still exercise considerable influence on the Prince of Wales. It is unlikely that his would have been among the few cautionary voices that doubted whether the youthful Lady Diana Spencer was the ideal bride for Prince Charles, but his obvious goodwill, his ability to give sensible opinions about the private life of anyone except himself and his remarkable capacity to communicate with those fifty years or more his junior meant that he might have been able to make a real contribution to the married happiness of the heir to the throne.

Such a contribution was to be sorely needed. In the short term the Prince of Wales's wedding seemed spectacularly to revive the fortunes of the monarchy. Princess Diana's youth, beauty, charm and astonishing capacity to communicate with others seemed unmitigated assets. The royal wedding in July 1981 was the subject of vast public interest and the almost overwhelming attention of the media. It was treated as an occasion that far transcended the boundaries of ordinary human relationships. 'This is the stuff of which fairy tales are made,' pronounced the Archbishop of Canterbury. More pertinently, he went on to say: 'Those who are married live happily ever after the wedding day if they persevere in the real adventure, which is the royal task of creating each other and creating a more loving world.' Few of those present thought to question whether the couple would indeed persevere in that real adventure, but the Queen for one must have been uneasily conscious of the fact that her son and his young wife were almost entirely incompatible, with different interests, different tastes, different friends, and only the frailest framework of romance to bind them together.

The royal wedding had fanned to hurricane force the attention that the media lavished on the royal family. The trouble, of course, was that the press was not going to be satisfied for long with accounts of fairy-tale romances or cosy domesticity. If there were imperfections, they would be ruthlessly exposed: scandals were what was wanted – if they did not exist, they would have to be invented or, at least, richly embroidered. The Prince of Wales himself soon became a controversial figure. Instead of contenting himself with opening hospitals and oozing amiable platitudes, he showed that he had strong views on a variety of subjects and would not hesitate to voice them. Usually those views were sensible, sometimes they were remarkably prescient, but he made enemies and was denounced for interference and making improper use of the influence bestowed by his position. An interest in alternative medicines and a rash remark about talking to his flowers led to his dismissal as a fantastical crank. Even before his marriage began visibly to disintegrate, large sections of the British public had been led to view him with some suspicion and to question his fitness to become King.

But it was his younger siblings who did most to damage the royal image. Prince Andrew, created Duke of York on the day of his wedding in July 1986, had seemed previously to be the licensed jester of the royal family. 'Randy Andy', as he was styled by the popular press, was known to favour a rackety lifestyle, but his relationship with the actress Koo Stark was viewed with tolerant amusement and his service with the Falklands Task Force did wonders for his reputation. But his marriage to Sarah Ferguson was to provide rich fodder for the tabloids. The Queen must have felt that Miss Ferguson – horsey, jolly, open-air and notably insensitive – was in many ways better cut out than Diana Spencer to marry into the royal family. But she was also 'vulgar, vulgar, vulgar', as Martin Charteris in an unguarded moment described her, 'not cut out to be a royal princess in this or any other age'. The house that the Yorks built together, Sunninghill Park, vast and spectacularly tasteless, offended the more discriminating by its gracelessness and everyone else by its extravagance. Soon the marriage was on the rocks, with the Duchess of York taking little trouble to conceal her conspicuous philandering with men who would have been unsuitable as friends, let alone as lovers.

Prince Edward was next to contribute to the general malaise. His decision to abandon the Royal Marines and take up a career in theatre management was a courageous one, but it reinforced the public perception of him as being something of a quitter, dim and slightly wet. His theatrical career did not flourish and in 1987 he was responsible for one of the most embarrassing episodes in which his family can ever have been involved: the royal 'It's a Knockout' television programme. This well-intentioned effort to raise money for charity involved Prince Edward, the Yorks and the normally ultra-sensible Princess Anne in a series of catastrophically unfunny antics. To crown the debacle, Prince Edward totally misjudged the mood of a group of journalists, who had been cooped up for hours without even a drop of alcohol to cheer them, and stumped out peevishly when they failed to show sufficient, or indeed any, enthusiasm. Princess Anne must surely have joined in this enterprise against her better judgment. She was the most admirably conscientious of royal princesses, but her own marriage was in trouble and five years later she was divorced. In retrospect, it is easy to say that the Queen should have intervened at an early stage to veto the royal 'Knockout', but she was always reluctant to exert authority within the family and seems rarely to have played a significant part in any of the imbroglios in which her children were involved.

However seriously the reputations of her children might be affected, the Queen herself survived more or less inviolate. When a spectator fired six shots at her at the ceremony of Trooping the Colour in 1981 and an intruder, Michael Fagan, succeeded in penetrating as far as her bedroom in Buckingham Palace early one morning in 1982, she behaved with calm and courage. In fact the bullets proved to be blanks and Fagan a harmless idiot, but in both cases she had reason to believe that she was in serious danger. The British people were reinforced in their belief that she was a woman of conspicuous quality.

That the political importance of her role was, nevertheless, continuing to diminish was shown in November 1990 when Mrs Thatcher accepted the inevitable and stood down as prime minister. When Harold Macmillan had been hurried, if not harried, from office in 1963, the Queen had found herself called on to play a vital part in the selection of his successor; on this occasion the new procedures for the election of a leader for the Tory Party worked smoothly and she was required to do no more than formally to endorse the succession of John Major. Undoubtedly she was relieved at not being called on to make difficult decisions; equally, the fact that she was acting as no more than a rubber stamp fortified the arguments of those who claimed that the monarchy was an expensive luxury that the country could ill afford and that offered little if any value for the money involved.

It was the cost of the monarchy that did most to weaken the position of the Queen in the last decades of the twentieth century. The increase in the Civil List, from just over £5 million a year to just under £8 million, which Mrs Thatcher had pushed through shortly before her political demise, had been intended to settle the question of the royal finances for a decade at least. So, up to a point, it did, but the national mood was becoming more and more critical of anything that seemed like extravagance in any walk of public life, and the occasional excesses of the younger royals led to enquiries as to whether the whole apparatus of the monarchy was not unnecessarily lavish. Still more dangerous, the impression grew that the Queen was fabulously rich and could easily afford to bear some of the expenses that a hard-pressed nation was shouldering on her behalf. If the Crown Jewels, the Royal Collection of paintings, drawings and priceless artefacts, the development value of Buckingham Palace and its gardens, were thrown into the pot, then the Queen was indeed fabulously rich, but in terms of disposable income she was a wealthy but not enormously wealthy woman. She – or her advisers – were, however, reluctant to expose the true extent of her fortune and this, coupled with the fact that she was exempt from income tax, meant that the republicans were able to make much play with the image of bloated parasites growing fat at the expense of the nation and even made loyal monarchists admit that some consideration of the royal finances was overdue. In the end she got the worst of both worlds: when it was announced in November 1992 that the Queen had agreed in future to pay tax on her private income and to reimburse the Civil List for annuities paid to various members of the royal family, the press presented the decision as being a belated surrender to overwhelming public opinion and complained that she was still exempt from inheritance tax.

It must have seemed to the Queen that things could get no worse. '1992 is not a year on which I shall look back with undiluted pleasure,' she remarked in a speech at Guildhall. 'In the words of one of my more sympathetic correspondents, it has turned out to be an *annus horribilis*.' It seemed that everything had conspired to cause her distress. The most conspicuous, if not the most painful, disaster had been the fire at Windsor Castle. Major renovations were being carried out, so most of the more fragile works of art were safely out of harm's way, but the damage to the structure was massive and St George's Hall was entirely gutted. Photographs of the Queen forlornly surveying the wreckage of her beloved home won the nation's sympathy, but the mood quickly changed. Peter Brooke, the Heritage Secretary, announced that the government would bear the full costs of the repairs – estimated to be in the neighbourhood of £50 million. He had deluded himself that this decision would command popular approval, but instead there was an outburst of indignation – fomented if not created by the press. This was the Queen's home, it was argued; why should she not, like her subjects, have insured against disaster? Anyway, she could well afford to pay for the repairs herself. The fact that the royal apartments were untouched and that the damaged rooms were used only for state occasions was not deemed to be relevant. In the end it was decided that the Queen would herself foot the bill and seek to recoup some of the cost by opening Buckingham Palace to the public. As with the agreement to pay income tax, the announcement was treated not as a generous gesture but as a belated surrender to popular pressure.

The Queen pictured on 21 November 1992 inspecting the damage caused by the fire at Windsor Castle.

But it was once more the misfortunes of the royal children that earned the most hostile attention. The Yorks separated after the Duchess had been guilty of some spectacularly vulgar and well-publicized indiscretions with a rich American playboy. Princess Anne's marriage was dissolved – a denouement conducted with dignity on both sides but still contributing to the picture of a fractured and faltering royal family. It was, however, the wreck of the marriage of the Prince of Wales that did the greatest damage. It had been increasingly obvious over the previous years that the couple were finding it difficult to co-exist with even the most inadequate simulacrum of domestic harmony. They appeared less and less often in public together; when they did, it was painfully obvious that they hardly related to each other. Princess Diana proved herself uniquely skilled at manipulating the media: in February 1992 the photograph of her sitting, soulful and conspicuously alone, in front of the Taj Mahal, that supreme monument to marital love, was worth a hundred newspaper stories arguing her side of the story.

It was a book published in the summer of 1992, Andrew Morton's *Diana: Her True Story*, that did the greatest damage. The title was justified in that the story was not actually untrue, but it was monstrously unfair in that it so obviously presented only one side of the affair. The author claimed that it was based on sources very close to the Princess of Wales; it is to his credit that only much later did it become clear that the most important source was the Princess herself. It painted a picture of a warm-hearted and impulsive woman kept at bay by a cold and unresponsive husband and treated with suspicious distaste by an introverted family who regarded her as a loose cannon to be, if possible, neutralized by any means, fair or foul. They could not understand why Diana would not conform to the rules and were outraged by what they saw as her intemperate exhibitionism. Allegations that the Prince of Wales had been unfaithful from an early stage of the relationship were reserved for later, but nothing was spared to depict him as being incapable of giving his wife the support and love that she craved. The Queen herself was treated cautiously – the Princess went out of her way to insist that she had 'a deep respect' for her mother-in-law – but there was no suggestion that she had taken any noticeable step to help Diana through her difficulties or to urge her son to take his marital duties more seriously.

Morton's book must have convinced the Queen that there was not even the smallest chance that the relationship could be patched up, and that in the long run a clean break would be better than embittered and long-drawn-out guerilla warfare. At the end of 1995 she wrote both to her son and to Princess Diana to advise them that they should start proceedings for a divorce. The fairy-tale romance was finally ended, but the aftershocks were to cause even more damage than the original eruption.

It is a truism among those versed in public relations that, if there is good news, it should be eked out and fed to the world drop by drop. In the case of bad news, however, it should be concentrated in as short a period as possible. There was very little design behind the misfortunes that smote the monarchy in the last decade of the twentieth century, but at least the propagandists could congratulate themselves that the bad news had indeed come all together; recuperation could now begin. In fact, there was one more violent convulsion to come in which the Queen would find herself dangerously involved, but, as the years slipped away after the *annus horribilis*, it seemed that the worst might be over. The Queen would be seventy-three when the new millennium dawned. She had weathered the middle years; now she could advance into what history suggested might be the calmer waters of old age.

In 1977 the Queen celebrated twenty-five years on the throne. This photograph was taken for the Silver Jubilee tour of the Pacific in the spring of that year. The Queen is in the Throne Room at Buckingham Palace on the day of the State Opening of Parliament in November 1976. The white silk dress by Norman Hartnell was first worn for the opening of Sydney Opera House in 1973 – the pattern of the gold and silver embroidery was designed to reflect the roofline of that innovative building. *Peter Grugeon*

The Queen with her first grandson, Peter Phillips, who was born in November 1977. The photograph was issued the following April to mark the Queen's fifty-second birthday. *Snowdon*

The royal family at Balmoral in 1979, with Princess Anne's son, Peter Phillips, the centre of attention.

The Queen on the balcony of Buckingham Palace with the
Prince and Princess of Wales after their wedding on 29 July 1981.
'This is the stuff of which fairy tales are made,' pronounced
the Archbishop of Canterbury. *Lionel Cherruault*

The immediate families photographed in the Throne Room after
the marriage of Prince Charles and Lady Diana Spencer, 29 July
1981. Lord Lichfield used a referee's whistle to obtain everyone's
attention at the beginning of the forty-minute session.

A rarely seen photograph of the Queen, taken in 1982 during the setting-up for portraits to be used as Royal Mail stamps. *Snowdon*

The Prince and Princess of Wales with the Queen, Queen Elizabeth the Queen Mother and Prince William after the christening of Prince Harry in St George's Chapel, Windsor, on 21 December 1984. *Snowdon*

OVERLEAF Karsh took a series of photographs for a royal tour of Canada in 1984. It was more than forty years since his first photograph of the Queen, taken in 1943.

OPPOSITE AND ABOVE Further pictures taken
for the 1984 Canadian tour in which the Queen
is wearing Canadian orders. *Karsh*

Prince Andrew's portrait of the Queen taken at
Sandringham for her sixtieth birthday in April 1986.

OVERLEAF Prince Andrew's wedding to Sarah Ferguson
in July 1986. Albert Watson, a fashion photographer
based in New York, took the official photographs.

207

Karsh's photograph of the Queen and the Duke of Edinburgh
at Balmoral with their four eldest grandchildren was used
by the royal couple for their personal Christmas card in 1987.
The four children are Prince William (left), Prince Harry (centre),
Peter Phillips (standing at the back) and Zara Phillips (right).

Terry O'Neill, who took this picture of the Queen and the Duke
of Edinburgh at Sandringham in February 1992, is particularly
known for his photographs of Hollywood film stars.

At the same session, in February 1992, O'Neill secured
these two spectacularly happy pictures of the Queen.
It was the fortieth anniversary of her accession to the throne.

Another of Terry O'Neill's 1992 photographs of the Queen
and the Duke of Edinburgh at Sandringham. This was taken
at the beginning of the year that the Queen later referred to
as her *annus horribilis*.

The Queen in February 1996, shortly before
her seventieth birthday. *Brian Aris*

IV

NEW MILLENNIUM, OLD MONARCHY

1997–2011

One of the photographs taken for the
Queen's Golden Jubilee was this image by the
Australian-born photographer Polly Borland.

The Prince of Wales's disastrous marriage was to continue to wreak havoc in the royal family long after the couple had finally separated. Even if the press had been ready to treat the Waleses' problems with a modicum of reticence, Princess Diana was too fond of the limelight and felt far too bitterly towards her husband and his family to let the matter drop. She, far more than the Prince, was the focal point of the press's attention, and she would not have had it otherwise. In the first six days of March 1993 alone, three and a half thousand column inches in the national newspapers were devoted to Diana and her doings. The Prince of Wales had to make do with less than a tenth as much. He did not let his side of the story go untold – in a long television interview and a subsequent biography Jonathan Dimbleby put forth his side of the case with considerable skill, and with what some felt to be an embarrassing richness of detail – but the Princess easily out-performed him in her public appearances. These culminated in the now discredited 'Panorama' interview of November 1995 in which her carefully nuanced grief, her confessions of guilt skilfully couched so as to make it clear that she was far more sinned against than sinning, were seen by 22 million people and did untold damage to what was left of the reputation of the Prince of Wales. It must have been this broadcast more than any other single factor that led the Queen to urge divorce on her son and daughter-in-law. On 28 August 1996 the divorce became final. Diana could no longer style herself Her Royal Highness; on the other hand, her assiduous lawyers ensured that, even though she had to sink back to the level of a commoner, it was a commoner endowed with a fortune of £17 million.

She lived to enjoy it for little more than a year. On 31 August 1997 the car in which she was travelling with her Egyptian lover, Dodi Al Fayed, crashed in the Place de l'Alma road tunnel in Paris. The chauffeur had been drinking heavily and was driving at great speed so as to escape the paparazzi on motorcycles who had pursued the couple from the Ritz hotel where they had been dining. Dodi's father, Mohamed Al Fayed, would not accept that this was the case. The 'accident', he claimed, had in fact been murder, perpetrated by British Intelligence at the behest of the Duke of Edinburgh, who was horrified at the thought of the mother of the future King marrying a Muslim. No one except a few crazed conspiracy theorists believed this fantasy, but it was not until 2008 that the legend was at last put to rest when an inquest found that the accident had indeed been the result of reckless driving. Al Fayed finally dropped his case. His suspicions had done little if any harm to the royal family, but the immediate aftermath of the death of Princess Diana did more to shake the standing of the monarchy than any event since the abdication.

An overwhelming tide of grief swept over the British people. Some maintained that it had been whipped up by the press and was a hysterical and largely spurious reaction. No one, however, who watched the millions of mourners – stable, normal, respectable mothers and fathers with their children – making their pilgrimage to leave their tributes at one of the sites with which Diana was associated can doubt that their feelings were real and strongly felt. In death even more than in life, the 'People's Princess' possessed the ability to touch the public's deepest feelings.

Her sons, the young Princes William and Harry, were at Balmoral. The Queen's instinct as a grandmother was to protect them from the worst of the fall-out from their mother's death, to stay with them in Scotland and let them grieve in private, maintaining a life as close as possible to normality. The nation did not see it that way. They expected a public affirmation of grief from their monarch. The fact that the flagpole above Buckingham Palace, from which the royal standard flew when the Queen was in residence, remained bare, caused particular offence. This was as tradition dictated, but the people were not interested in tradition. They wanted a flag at half-mast, they wanted the Queen to lead the national mourning. There was a mood of popular anger against the monarchy such as Britain had rarely seen before. To the royal advisers it seemed briefly as if the very future of the throne was insecure.

The Queen and the Duke of Edinburgh on 5 September 1997, surrounded by flowers left outside Buckingham Palace following the death of Diana, Princess of Wales.

The moment quickly passed. The Queen returned to London. The Union flag was flown at half-mast above Buckingham Palace. The Queen and Prince Philip appeared in front of the Palace, marvelling at the mountains of flowers, cards and teddy bears that had accumulated in the Princess's honour. On 5 September, on the eve of the funeral, the Queen spoke to the nation on television. Diana, she said, had been 'an exceptional and gifted human … who made many, many people happy'. She praised her daughter-in-law for her energy and her commitment to others, especially for her devotion to her two boys. Most crucially, she admitted: 'I, for one, believe there are lessons to be drawn from her life and from the extraordinary and moving reaction to her death.' It was a singularly well-judged and moving declaration; instantly it defused the worst of the public's rancour. Queen and nation were as one again.

There was another sting in the tail, however. In October 2002 Paul Burrell, the Princess's butler and confidant, who had made rich pickings out of exploiting in print his relationship with his former employer, was put on trial for stealing a large number of personal effects that had belonged to the Princess or to the Prince of Wales and the children. At the last minute the case collapsed because the Queen remembered that, shortly after Diana's death, she had been told by Burrell that he had taken certain items of Princess Diana's to his home so as to make sure that they were looked after properly. Inevitably this belated recollection caused some surprise. Had the Queen really forgotten the conversation with Burrell or did she fear that, if the trial was continued, even more dirty linen would be washed in public and her grandchildren caused still greater grief? Burrell's own recollection of his meeting with the Queen does not carry total conviction. Their conversation had lasted nearly three hours, he alleged, and at the end of it the Queen had warned: 'Be careful, Paul. There are powers at work in this country about which we have no knowledge.' It is hard to see that any such 'powers at work' would have been particularly interested in the activities of Princess Diana's butler, however indiscreet and self-seeking he might have been; it is supremely unlikely that the Queen should have indulged in so opaquely sinister a pronouncement.

***

The events following Diana's death figured largely in a film called *The Queen*, produced in 2006, in which Helen Mirren played Queen Elizabeth II. It is said that Mirren started making the film as a republican and ended it as a fervent monarchist. Whether this is true or not, her representation of the Queen is uncommonly convincing and almost entirely sympathetic. In the film, a large part of the credit for persuading the Queen that it was essential for her to leave Balmoral and come south to join in the nation's mourning is given to Prime Minister Tony Blair. Certainly he played a large part in the debate, and the monarchy owes him a debt for his efforts. Blair had only recently become prime minister. As Leader of the Opposition he had made it his business to occupy the political middle ground, an enterprise of which the Queen must heartily have approved. Blair was articulate, intelligent, charming almost to a fault; it is said, however, that he gave the impression in Buckingham Palace that, while he was properly respectful of the Head of State, he did not rate the monarchy particularly high in his scale of priorities. The time of the weekly royal audience was altered to suit his convenience: the request for the change was made with suitable deference but it was still clear that the demands made on him by parliamentary questions bulked larger in his mind than his weekly hour with the Queen.

Even though the actual decommissioning of *Britannia* took place when he was prime minister, Blair was in no way responsible for the decision to abandon the royal yacht. *Britannia* had been in service for forty-four years and, if justification for its replacement was needed on purely economic grounds, a good case could have been based on the contribution it made to the promotion of British exports by providing a uniquely splendid venue for the entertainment of foreign dignitaries. The political will was lacking, however; the Conservative Chancellor, Norman Lamont, argued strongly against the building of another royal yacht, the opportunity was missed. The Queen attended *Britannia*'s formal decommissioning on a bleak winter's day in December 1997. It was one of the few occasions in her life when she allowed herself to display emotion; photographs of the event showed her and the Princess Royal with tears in their eyes.

Inevitably the dawn of a new millennium involved the Queen in a host of events and ceremonial openings linked, however tenuously, to the occasion. Most conspicuous was the spectacularly ill-organized celebration at the Millennium Dome in east London – an occasion that saw VIPs from all over Britain queuing disconsolately for several hours on New

The Queen and Prince Charles at the paying-off ceremony for the royal yacht *Britannia* at Portsmouth, 11 December 1997. Launched in 1953, the ship had travelled over one million miles on 968 official voyages.

Year's Eve. Compared with them, the Queen escaped quite lightly, but she cannot have got much pleasure from her night at the Dome. For several years the building threatened to be an alarmingly expensive white elephant; at least some of the other millennium-related projects promised to be more useful. She opened, *inter alia*, the Millennium Link, a canal restoration scheme that made it possible to travel by boat across central Scotland; a Millennium coastal park in Carmarthenshire; a Millennium bridge at Gateshead; Millennium Point, a multi-use complex in Birmingham costing in excess of £114 million; not to mention a Millennium Royal Tattoo, a Millennium Royal Variety Performance and a wide range of other such activities at which her presence was deemed desirable if not essential. For a woman of seventy-three it was heavy going, but it was no more than a trial run for the Golden Jubilee that was due two years later.

The year 2002 started sadly, with the deaths within a couple of months of Princess Margaret and the Queen Mother. Princess Margaret was only seventy-one, but she had been ill for several years. The loss of one's only sibling is always likely to be a harrowing experience; for the Queen, who had so few people in her life with whom she could totally relax, it must have been particularly painful. She had little time to mourn, however; three days after the funeral she was in Jamaica for the first of her Jubilee tours. The welcome was warm, the crowds enthusiastic, the occasion made memorable by a power-cut at the Governor General's house just before the farewell banquet. The Queen groped her way to the table; dinner was eaten by candlelight while cars outside the windows shone their headlights into the dining room. Ten days later she was in Australia and then on to New Zealand. The visit to both countries was another tumultuous success; in Brisbane thirty thousand people gathered in the rain to hear her speak. Four weeks later the Queen Mother died. She was 101 years old and with her died an extraordinary link with the beginnings of the twentieth century. The queue for her lying-in-state in Westminster Hall stretched for more than three miles, and a million people lined the funeral route. 'These are days for republicans to walk humbly,' wrote the journalist Jonathan Freedland in the *Guardian*. As Queen Mary had done at the time of the Coronation, Queen Elizabeth timed her death with exquisite consideration for others. Saddened though the Queen must have been at the death of her mother, the formal mourning was over by the time that the celebration of the Golden Jubilee in Britain really got under way in June.

Viewed in historical terms the Golden Jubilee was, indeed, an occasion to be celebrated. In 2002 Elizabeth became the third longest-reigning British monarch and the second longest-reigning monarch still on earth (King Bhumibol of Thailand was narrowly ahead of her). To displace Victoria as the longest-reigning British monarch she would have to wait until 2015 (she would overtake George III in 2012, and he anyway had cheated since there had been a regency during the last ten years of his reign).

Even without this, however, it was evident that her reign had been of remarkable length. But did longevity count for anything? As usual there were predictions that the Golden Jubilee would prove to be a non-event; as usual, when the time came, the public reaction proved to be riotously enthusiastic. The most spectacular event was the Prom at the Palace. Two million people applied for tickets; twelve thousand crowded into the garden of Buckingham Palace. Two days later occurred a still more unprecedented event. The Party at the Palace featured, among others, Paul McCartney, Eric Clapton, Cliff Richard and Tony Bennett. The Queen guitarist, Brian May, started the proceedings by playing his arrangement of 'God Save the Queen' from the Palace roof. Once again there were twelve thousand people in the gardens and this time a million or more on the Mall. At the end of the concert the Queen lit a National Beacon at the Victoria Memorial – the last of a chain of beacons that, as had happened at the Golden Jubilee of Queen Victoria, had been lit around the world.

The heart of the Jubilee was the National Service of Thanksgiving at St Paul's. The Archbishop of Canterbury quoted a sentence from the Golden Speech of Queen Elizabeth I, which she had delivered to the members of the House of Commons in 1601: 'Though God hath raised me high, I count the glory of my Crown that I have reigned with your loves.' The Queen might have uttered the words herself and spoken with the same sincerity as her august predecessor. At the Guildhall banquet that followed the service, the Queen offered her heartfelt thanks to 'every one of you – here in Guildhall, those of you waiting in the Mall and the streets of London, and all those up and down this country and throughout the Commonwealth, who may be watching this on television. Thank you all for your enthusiasm to mark and celebrate these past fifty years. Gratitude, respect and pride, these words sum up how I feel about the people of this country and the Commonwealth – and what this Golden Jubilee means to me.'

The Queen at the Prom at the Palace held on 1 June 2002 as part of the Golden Jubilee celebrations. Over twelve thousand members of the public and many members of the royal family attended the concert in the garden of Buckingham Palace.

The fact that she mentioned the Commonwealth twice in her peroration is an indication of how large it bulked in her consciousness. The same could not be said of most of her ministers. Blair did not have the same distaste for the Commonwealth as had been true of Heath and Thatcher, but he was far more concerned about the 'special relationship' with the United States and left to himself would have done little to foster ties within the former Empire. Sometimes it must have seemed to the Queen as if she was the only person left who truly had the cause of the Commonwealth at heart. Yet it included nearly two billion people, a third of the world's population, and counted fifty-three countries among its members. It was second only to the United Nations in its scope and, unlike the United Nations, professed (if it did not always perfectly practise) certain common ideals and a code of conduct.

'The Commonwealth', said the Queen on its sixtieth anniversary in March 2009, 'to me has been sustained … by the continuity of our mutual values and goals. Our beliefs in freedom, democracy and human rights; equality and equity; and development and prosperity mean as much today as they did more than half a century ago. These values come from a common responsibility exercised by our governments and peoples. It is this which makes the Commonwealth a family of nations and peoples, at ease with being together.' That she was Queen of only a few of its members was to her a matter of small concern. In spite of the warm welcome Australia had given her on her Jubilee tour, she accepted that it was probable, perhaps inevitable, that within a few years it would declare itself a republic. New Zealand and Canada might survive as monarchies, if only because they wished to distinguish themselves from Australia in the first place and the United States in the second, but here too she would accept the contrary with equanimity. It was the continuation of the Commonwealth that mattered and if, as its Head, she could do something to strengthen its cohesion, then that something would be done.

The fact that the Commonwealth was divided on the merits of intervention in Iraq and Afghanistan must have given her some reason to question the wisdom of Blair's determination to back the Americans in their enterprises. Still more, her knowledge of imperial history must have led her to question the practicality even more than the legitimacy of these wars. As always, she gave no public indication of her views; we will probably never know whether she merely listened when Blair expounded the allied strategy or hinted at certain doubts.

She had a very personal reason to follow the fighting in Afghanistan with anxious attention for, from December 2007, her grandson Prince Harry had been serving there as a forward air controller. His presence in Afghanistan had been kept secret, for if it had been known that he was there, he would have been a prime target for enemy activity and have not merely been at great risk himself but would have imperilled the lives of his colleagues around him. At the end of February 2008 an American website revealed his whereabouts; to his chagrin he was at once recalled. As complaints mounted about the inadequate logistic support given to the British forces in Afghanistan, the Queen must have felt herself pulled apart. As Head of the Armed Forces she felt responsibility for every serviceman in the British ranks; as Queen she could speak only with the voice of her ministers. It is unlikely that, even in the most confidential conclave, she committed herself to any criticism of her government's behaviour; equally it is certain that her prime minister was left in no doubt about her hope that everything possible would be done to sustain her soldiers in the field.

By then she had a new prime minister to contend with. In June 2007 Blair finally stood down in favour of his long-standing friend, rival and colleague, Gordon Brown. Once again the Queen's role was purely formal, but it still meant a great deal to the new incumbent. 'It's not every day', he said, 'that you meet the Queen at 1.30 p.m., become the Prime Minister at 2 p.m., speak to the [US] President at 3 p.m., and get told by Sarah to put the kids to bed at 7 p.m.' The last part of that comment must have struck the Queen with particular force. No one had ever told her to put the kids to bed: perhaps she would have rather liked it if they had.

Economic storm clouds were looming by the time Brown moved into Number 10 and within a few months the country was embroiled in a full-blooded crisis and the sharpest recession for many years. An elaborate diamond-wedding party to be held at the Ritz had been planned for April 2008; the Queen felt that this was no time for conspicuous jollification and called it off. But while it was relatively easy to cancel a single party, it was more difficult to change a way of life. The fat that had been accumulated during the years in which the Civil List had yielded an excess of income over expenditure had been eaten away. Within two or three years, perhaps even sooner, the monarchy would either have to receive a substantially increased Civil List or drastically to cut down on its activities and standard of living. Some further economies, of course, could and would be made, but the essential problem remained. No one, or very few at any rate, wanted an end to garden parties, investitures and state banquets, or to see the closure of the Royal Mews or the sale of Sandringham; yet could the Queen possibly ask for a substantial pay increase at a time when her people were being told that they would have to pay higher taxes, accept a deterioration in public services and count themselves lucky if they had a job at all, let alone enjoyed an annual increment to keep them ahead of the cost of living?

Pressures to reduce government expenditure on the Civil List had been increasing for many years, thanks to lobbying both in Parliament by republican-minded politicians and in the news media, not only in the United Kingdom but across the Commonwealth. Finally, it was a Conservative Chancellor, George Osborne, who announced the abolition of the list in 2011. The Civil List Act of 1760 – which directed that the hereditary revenues from the

Crown Estate were to be paid to Parliament, which would in turn defray the expenses of the Royal Household – now yielded to the new Sovereign Grant Act, under which a single grant was to be determined annually. It was modernization, of a sort, that responded to a national mood critical of the seemingly lavish lifestyle of the royal family; the Queen's agreement in 1992 to pay tax on her private income had not entirely placated anti-monarchist critics.

As the Queen entered her ninth decade, the stresses and strains that afflict the ageing body began to tell. In 2006 troubles with her back led to the cancellation of her opening of Arsenal football club's new Emirates Stadium in London. It even seemed possible that she would be unable to open Parliament: she managed it, but only, it was obvious, at the price of considerable discomfort. A bandaged hand led to suggestions that she was receiving an intravenous drip to combat osteoporosis; in fact she had only been nipped by a royal corgi, but the incident reminded people how vulnerable even the most healthy and cosseted old lady must be. A badly bloodshot eye implied a burst blood vessel, which in its turn pointed to high blood pressure. Nobody could replace her in her relationship with the prime minister or with the Commonwealth leaders, and nothing would stop her wading through the massive dossier of papers with which she was each day confronted, but she began to ease off. She started to travel less, and to leave an increasing number of royal duties to the Prince of Wales or other members of her family.

The Queen made it abundantly clear on several occasions that she would not contemplate abdication, a possibility that was rumoured by some journalists and commentators. 'It's not like a normal job, it's a job for life,' said Margaret Rhodes, the Queen's first cousin and long-time lady-in-waiting to her mother, who probably knew her as well as anyone except the Duke of Edinburgh. The Coronation vows, once made, were irrevocable: 'She would not consider not continuing to fulfil those vows until she dies.' Despite her advancing years, the nation heartily continued to support this resolution. The Queen's presence in Buckingham Palace remained a symbol of continuity, of stability. The very fact that she lacked the charismatic glamour of her former daughter-in-law, Princess Diana, was in a curious way an asset. The Queen was appreciated in a different way: she was still a link with the past, the fount of wisdom – real or fancied – based on infinite experience.

In April 2011 the public mood was lifted by the wedding at Westminster Abbey of the Queen's grandson. Prince William, second in line to the throne after his father, was married to Catherine Middleton in a service watched live by some 36 million viewers in the United Kingdom, and tens of millions more around the world. The bride wore a tiara lent by the Queen and the sapphire and diamond engagement ring that had once belonged to Diana, Princess of Wales; inevitably, the presence of this ring brought memories of Charles and Diana's 'fairy-tale' wedding back to the surface. The couple – now created Duke and Duchess of Cambridge – succeeded in creating a powerful public memory of their own, with colourful photographs updating (if not eclipsing) the famous photograph of William's parents on the balcony at Buckingham Palace.

A state visit by the Queen in 2011 to the Republic of Ireland marked a conciliatory moment in the troubled history of relations between the two countries. Almost one hundred years had passed since Elizabeth's grandfather George V had toured Ireland in 1911, ten years before the partition of the island into two self-governing polities, the larger of which had declared itself a free state in 1922. In a speech at Dublin Castle in May, the Queen acknowledged the country's turbulent history, adding: 'With the benefit of historical hindsight we can all see things which we would wish had been done differently or not at all.' In June 2012, during her Diamond Jubilee year, many people on both sides of the Irish Sea would be amazed to see the Queen shake hands with Martin McGuinness, Sinn Féin's deputy first minister and a former senior member of the IRA, the very organization that had claimed responsibility for the death of Lord Mountbatten, a distant cousin of the Queen, in 1979. The handshake – unthinkable for many, thirty years on – represented a moment of remarkable bravery on both sides, recalling something of the spirit of reconciliation marked by the Good Friday Agreement, an emotional and hard-won step in the Northern Ireland peace process, signed in 1998 but still fresh in the memory. It demonstrated that while the monarchy stood for continuity, it did not mean that history stood still.

This photograph of the Queen and the Duke of Edinburgh was taken in the White Drawing Room at Buckingham Palace by Brian Aris to mark their golden wedding anniversary in November 1997. Lord Snowdon's less formal picture opposite was taken at about the same time.

The wedding of Lady Sarah Armstrong-Jones, the Queen's niece,
to the actor Daniel Chatto took place in July 1994. *Robin Matthews*

Five years later, in June 1999, Prince Edward married Sophie Rhys-Jones in
St George's Chapel, Windsor, and was created Earl of Wessex. On the advice
of his brother-in-law, Lord Lichfield, the photographer Sir Geoffrey Shakerley
took ten large copies of the *Yellow Pages* telephone directory to assist with
the height levels and recalled that 'that caused a certain amount of merriment'.

Traditionally only one photographer at a time was invited to take official photographs for royal occasions, but for the Golden Jubilee of 2002 ten were called on. As his contribution to the portfolio, David Secombe, the son of the comedian Harry Secombe, took this photograph of the Queen working in the Regency Room at Buckingham Palace in November 2001.

Nearly fifty years after Beaton's famous Coronation photograph, a more relaxed Queen was portrayed in her Parliamentary robes in the Throne Room at Buckingham Palace, October 2001. *Julian Calder*

Four portraits of his mother by the Duke of York, taken
for the Golden Jubilee during the royal family's stay at
Sandringham, Christmas 2001.

The Canadian rock star and photographer Bryan Adams
took this charming portrait of the Queen in the informal
setting of a side entrance to Buckingham Palace. However,
it was not released as part of the Golden Jubilee portfolio
and is rarely seen.

A Golden Jubilee photograph taken by Lord Lichfield
at Buckingham Palace. It echoes Karsh's striking double
profile from the 1950s.

ABOVE AND OPPOSITE The Queen photographed by Lord Snowdon at his London studio for her eightieth birthday. The chair was designed by Lord Snowdon for the investiture of the Prince of Wales at Caernarfon Castle in 1969.

PREVIOUS PAGE Two eightieth-birthday portraits of the Queen in the Blue Drawing Room at Buckingham Palace, 2006. Jane Bown, the photographer, was particularly well known for her portraits of artists and authors. She used to say that she preferred to know little or nothing of her subjects – an advantage that was denied her in this case.

The Queen photographed by Lord Snowdon at Buckingham Palace in 2010, shortly before her eighty-fourth birthday.

V

THE FINAL DECADE

2012–2022

The Queen is photographed in 2010 wearing Canadian
orders and a maple brooch inherited from the Queen
Mother. *Julian Calder*

The year of the Queen's Diamond Jubilee coincided with the Olympic Games, held in London in the summer of 2012. The opening ceremony was like no other: it included a short film made at Buckingham Palace with the actor Daniel Craig, in character as the world's most celebrated British spy hero James Bond as he reported to the Sovereign for duty. He escorts the Queen to a helicopter, and in a perfect *coup de théâtre*, they appeared to parachute together into the Olympic stadium. The surprise was all the more successful for being perfectly kept, and the Queen demonstrated incontrovertibly that a strong sense of humour, so often hidden behind her public duties, was high among her personal qualities. In her willingness to participate – to be, in that most British of phrases, 'a good sport' – she won many hearts.

A sign that Elizabeth acknowledged her own advancing age was given shortly before her eighty-seventh birthday in 2013, when she missed the annual Commonwealth Day service for only the second time since ascending the throne sixty-one years earlier. It was announced that Charles would take her place, a clear indication of her 'sincere wish' – as she would state in 2018, shortly before the formal approval of Charles as Head of the Commonwealth – that her son should succeed her in the role. Her proven personal devotion to the Commonwealth – never in any doubt, in spite of the misgivings of others in the post-colonial age – was balanced against the demands of long-distance travel for a woman now well advanced into her tenth decade.

In July 2013, the Queen's third great-grandchild, George Alexander Louis, was born to the Duke and Duchess of Cambridge, third in line of succession to the throne after his grandfather Prince Charles and father Prince William. The royal baby's first name must undoubtedly have pleased the Queen, recalling that of her own father who had been crowned George VI. Prince George was the first member of the royal family since the reign of Queen Victoria to represent a third generation of heirs to the throne living at the same time.

One of the inevitable consequences of a long life is that the number of members of one's own age group dwindles. Not only was Elizabeth now the longest-lived and longest-reigning British monarch (she surpassed Queen Victoria in 2007 and 2015 respectively), in 2015 – on the death of King Abdullah of Saudi Arabia – she became the world's oldest monarch, and in 2016 – on the death of King Bhumibol of Thailand – the longest-serving head of state. These, however, may perhaps better be considered honourable milestones rather than honours in themselves. In 2017 Prince Philip stepped down after sixty-five years of official duties as the longest-serving royal consort in British history, another record-setting marker. In an important personal dimension, in the summer the couple celebrated their seventieth (platinum) wedding anniversary privately at Windsor Castle.

Late in 2019, a new threat arose that was unprecedented in scope and – for a brief period – seriously underestimated. Coronavirus disease (COVID-19), the often deadly manifestation of the most infectious virus of the modern era, began to be reported in Asia in December. Italy confirmed its first case in January 2020, and on 18 March the government of the United Kingdom announced it would close schools: on that day the Center for Systems Science and Engineering at Johns Hopkins University, Baltimore, credited as the authoritative source of data on the global pandemic, reported that cases worldwide numbered over 200,000. Five days later, the UK government imposed a national lockdown, ordering the population to stay at home for all but essential purposes. There followed months of restrictions on normal patterns of living and working, imposing great emotional hardship across the country; not to mention the impact of tens of thousands of deaths over and above the national average.

The Queen endured the imposition of new rules with the nation. Public engagements were cancelled, and she remained with her husband at Windsor Castle, within a strictly controlled sanitary cordon dubbed 'HMS Bubble'. In April she made a broadcast to the nation, acknowledging shared emotional trials: 'We should take comfort that while we may have more still to endure, better days will return: we will be with our friends again; we will be with our families again; we will meet again.' The allusion to that famous wartime song recalled the role her parents had played when they visited London's East End during the Blitz: a public show of solidarity and empathy from the monarch had then offered powerful comfort to a population under strain, and now did so again.

One year later, amid a continuing resurgence of the pandemic, and two months before his hundredth birthday, Prince Philip died at Windsor Castle. National mourning was made all the more acute by the poignant sight of the Queen sitting alone at his funeral, her isolation imposed by the current health regulations, which also obliged her, as all those attending, to wear a mask and not to sing. Although the Duke was widely held in the public's affection, it was the Queen for whom sympathy was palpably deepest. As she had said at her Golden Jubilee, 'He has, quite simply, been my strength and stay all these years.' After seventy-three years of marriage, she now contemplated life without him.

The Queen always acknowledged the strength she drew from her religious faith, and alluded to it in her last Christmas broadcast in 2021: 'for me and my family, even with one familiar laugh missing this year, there will be joy in Christmas, as we have the chance to reminisce, and see anew the wonder of the festive season through the eyes of our young children, of whom we were delighted to welcome four more this year. They teach us all a lesson – just as the Christmas story does – that in the birth of a child, there is a new dawn with endless potential. It is this simplicity of the Christmas story that makes it so universally appealing: simple happenings that formed the starting point of the life of Jesus – a man whose teachings have been handed down from generation to generation, and have been the bedrock of my faith.'

The Queen pictured at the Balmoral estate in Aberdeenshire for Julian Calder's photographic shoot (following pages). *Photograph Paul Whybrew / courtesy Julian Calder*

Despite precautions, the Queen contracted COVID-19 in February 2022, the month that marked her Platinum Jubilee; however, she recovered and undertook several duties. In April, she celebrated her ninety-sixth birthday. In May, she missed the State Opening of Parliament; her public appearances were now fewer and briefer, and on each occasion one could not help but notice her evident frailty. In June, the Archbishop of Canterbury Justin Welby visited the Queen at Windsor Castle. He later told the BBC, 'I came away thinking there is someone who has no fear of death, has hope in the future, knows the rock on which she stands and that gives her strength.'

On 6 September, the Queen appointed Liz Truss her fifteenth, and – although she would not know it – her shortest-serving, prime minister.

Two days later, on 8 September, at Balmoral, the Scottish estate that she had loved best of all, Queen Elizabeth died. At her side were her two eldest children, Charles and Anne. The long-arranged plans for her state funeral were set in motion, and eleven days later, in a series of impeccable ceremonies both regal and befitting Elizabeth's life of duty perfectly performed, she was interred next to her husband at St George's Chapel, Windsor.

An official Diamond Jubilee portrait of the Queen in 2012, marking the sixtieth anniversary of her accession. Photographed in the Centre Room at Buckingham Palace, the Queen is wearing a state dress by Angela Kelly, the State Diadem crown, and a collet necklace worn by Queen Victoria on her own Diamond Jubilee. On the blue Garter riband are the royal Family Orders of her grandfather, King George V (white ribbon), and her father, King George VI (pink ribbon), with the Garter star pinned below the sash. *John Swannell*

PREVIOUS PAGES The Queen by the Gelder Burn at the Balmoral estate, Aberdeenshire, in a photograph first released in 2013. She wears the robes of the Most Ancient and Most Noble Order of the Thistle, the greatest order of chivalry in Scotland, and insignia bearing the national flower. *Julian Calder*

The Queen in her office at Balmoral in 2011. *Julian Calder*

FOLLOWING PAGES The official portrait for the christening of Prince George Alexander Louis, photographed in the Morning Room at Clarence House, London, on 23 October 2013. Seated, from left to right, the Queen; Catherine, Duchess of Cambridge, holding Prince George; and William, Duke of Cambridge. Standing, from left to right, the Duke of Edinburgh, Prince Charles, Camilla Duchess of Cornwall and Prince Harry. Prince George is wearing a christening gown of delicate Honiton lace and white satin by Angela Kelly, an exact replica of one commissioned by Queen Victoria and worn by every baby born to the British royal family since 1841. *Jason Bell*

In a photograph marking the Diamond Jubilee in 2012,
the Queen is pictured with two of her horses in the grounds
of Windsor Castle. *Henry Dallal*

ABOVE A portrait taken in the White Drawing Room at Windsor
Castle to mark the Queen's seventieth anniversary as Colonel-in-
Chief of the 48th Highlanders of Canada. On her dress she wears
a platinum brooch set with diamonds, sapphires and rubies, which
was presented on her first visit to the regiment in 1951. A plaid in
the Davidson tartan of the 48th Highlanders of Canada is draped
over the chair. *Ian Leslie Macdonald*

OPPOSITE The Queen poses with three generations of her family:
Prince Charles, Prince William and Prince George. This photograph
was taken in the Throne Room at Buckingham Palace on 18 December
2019 and released in January 2020 to celebrate the start of a new
decade. *Ranald Mackechnie*

Two portraits of the Queen and the Duke of Edinburgh,
photographed at Windsor Castle, to celebrate their platinum
wedding anniversary in 2017. The Queen is wearing a cream
day dress by Angela Kelly and a gold 'scarab' brooch set with
rubies and diamonds, designed by Andrew Grima and given as a
personal gift from the Duke to the Queen in 1966. *Matt Holyoak*

The Queen at the Windsor Horse Show, in a photograph first
published on 21 April 2022 to mark her ninety-sixth birthday.
Henry Dallal

Chronology

The Photographers

Index

Acknowledgments

Credits

Chronology

1926

21 April Princess Elizabeth Alexandra Mary, daughter of the Duke and Duchess of York, granddaughter of George V and Queen Mary, born by Caesarean section at 17 Bruton Street, London w1, the home of her maternal grandparents, the Earl and Countess of Strathmore

29 May Princess Elizabeth christened in the private chapel, Buckingham Palace

1927

6 January–27 June Duke and Duchess of York visit New Zealand and Australia

1930

21 August Princess Margaret Rose born at Glamis Castle, Scotland

1933

January Alterations completed on Royal Lodge, Windsor Great Park, which had been granted to the Duke and Duchess of York as a country residence by George V in 1931. Y Bwythyn Bach (The Little House), a sixth-birthday gift to Princess Elizabeth from the people of Wales, was constructed in the grounds in 1932

Easter Marion Crawford becomes governess to Princess Elizabeth

1934

29 November Princess Elizabeth is a bridesmaid at the marriage of the Duke of Kent and Princess Marina of Greece

1936

20 January King George V dies and is succeeded by King Edward VIII

10 December King Edward VIII signs Instrument of Abdication. Succeeded by his brother the Duke of York who takes the title King George VI. The former king becomes the Duke of Windsor

1937

15 February Royal family moves from 145 Piccadilly and officially takes up residence at Buckingham Palace

12 May Coronation of George VI and Queen Elizabeth

28 May Neville Chamberlain becomes prime minister, succeeding fellow Conservative Stanley Baldwin

28 June It is announced that Princess Elizabeth is to become a Girl Guide

1938

27 September Princess Elizabeth accompanies Queen Elizabeth to launch the SS *Queen Elizabeth* at Clydebank

1939

17 May–15 June King George VI and Queen Elizabeth visit Canada and the USA. The first state visit to the United States by a reigning monarch

22 July Princess Elizabeth, with the royal family, visits the Royal Naval College at Dartmouth and meets Prince Philip of Greece

3 September War with Germany declared

1940

10 May Winston Churchill succeeds Neville Chamberlain as prime minister

12 May The two princesses are moved to Windsor Castle where they remain for most of the rest of the war

13 September The chapel at Buckingham Palace is destroyed in an air raid

13 October Princess Elizabeth gives first radio broadcast – to British children abroad

1942

24 February Princess Elizabeth becomes Colonel of the Grenadier Guards and on

21 April carries out her first official public engagement when she inspects detachments of the regiment at Windsor Castle

1943

February Princess Elizabeth is enrolled as a Sea Ranger

1944

21 April Princess Elizabeth turns eighteen and on 10 July makes the first appointment – a Lady in Waiting – to her own Household

22 July King George VI leaves for a tour of the Italian battlefields and appoints Princess Elizabeth a Counsellor of State prior to his departure. In his absence she carries out some of the duties of Head of State for the first time

1945

February Princess Elizabeth joins the ATS

8 May VE Day

5 July General election brings in Labour government under Clement Attlee

26 July Princess Elizabeth becomes a Junior Commander in the ATS

15 August VJ Day marks the end of the Second World War

1947

1 February–12 May The royal family visits southern Africa

18 March Prince Philip of Greece becomes a British citizen

21 April In a broadcast in South Africa on her twenty-first birthday, Princess Elizabeth dedicates herself to serve the Empire and Commonwealth

9 July Engagement of Princess Elizabeth and Lieutenant Philip Mountbatten, RN, is announced

11 November Princess Elizabeth appointed a Lady of the Garter by King George VI

20 November Marriage of Princess Elizabeth and HRH The Duke of Edinburgh in Westminster Abbey

1948

14 November Birth of Prince Charles at Buckingham Palace

15 December Christening of Prince Charles in the Music Room, Buckingham Palace

1949

26 April London Declaration establishes the modern Commonwealth

4 July Princess Elizabeth and the Duke of Edinburgh move into Clarence House, The Mall

1950

15 August Birth of Princess Anne at Clarence House

21 October Christening of Princess Anne in the Music Room, Buckingham Palace

1951

25 October Conservative Party under Sir Winston Churchill returns to power

8 October–17 November Princess Elizabeth and the Duke of Edinburgh visit Canada and the United States

1952

31 January Princess Elizabeth and the Duke of Edinburgh depart for Kenya and a tour of Australia and New Zealand

6 February King George VI dies in his sleep at Sandringham. Accession of Queen Elizabeth II

4 November The Queen's first State Opening of Parliament

1953

24 March Queen Mary dies

29 May Mount Everest conquered by Edmund Hillary and Tenzing Norgay

2 June Coronation of Queen Elizabeth II in Westminster Abbey

24 November The Queen and the Duke of Edinburgh begin a six-month Commonwealth tour to the West Indies, Pacific Islands, Australasia, Southeast Asia and Africa

1954

1 May The royal couple embark at Tobruk on the new royal yacht *Britannia* for the final leg of the Commonwealth tour. They are joined by Prince Charles and Princess Anne and arrive back in London on 15 May

1955

6 April Sir Anthony Eden succeeds Sir Winston Churchill as prime minister

31 October Princess Margaret publicly renounces marriage with Peter Townsend

1956

11 May First informal lunch party for distinguished guests from all professions, trades and vocations held at Buckingham Palace

26 July President Nasser of Egypt nationalizes the Suez Canal

29 October Israel, soon joined by British and French forces, attacks Egypt, initiating the Suez Crisis

1957

10 January Harold Macmillan succeeds Eden as prime minister

22 February HRH Philip, Duke of Edinburgh created a Prince of the United Kingdom by the Queen

August Lord Altrincham criticizes the Queen in *National and English Review*

25 December First televised Christmas message broadcast live from Sandringham House

1958

18, 19 and 20 March Last presentation of English debutantes at court

28 October State Opening of Parliament televised for the first time

1960

8 February Order-in-Council declares that descendants of the Queen not holding royal styles or titles should use the surname Mountbatten-Windsor

19 February Birth of Prince Andrew at Buckingham Palace

6 May Marriage of Princess Margaret and Antony Armstrong-Jones in Westminster Abbey

1961

6 October Antony Armstrong-Jones created Earl of Snowdon

3 November Birth of David, Viscount Linley, son of Princess Margaret and Lord Snowdon

9–20 November The Queen visits Ghana in spite of the doubts of the British government

1963

18 October Harold Macmillan resigns and is succeeded by Lord Home (subsequently Sir Alec Douglas-Home) as prime minister

1964

10 March Birth of Prince Edward at Buckingham Palace

1 May Birth of Lady Sarah Armstrong-Jones, daughter of Princess Margaret and Lord Snowdon

15 October Labour Party under Harold Wilson elected

1965

18–28 May The Queen and the Duke of Edinburgh make their first State Visit to the Federal Republic of Germany

October The Queen makes a personal appeal to Ian Smith, Prime Minister of Rhodesia, in an effort to avert a Unilateral Declaration of Independence

11 November Rhodesia declares UDI

1966

February–July Prince Charles spends two terms at Timbertop (part of Geelong Grammar School), Australia

29 October The Queen and the Duke of Edinburgh visit Aberfan, South Wales, after a slag heap collapses, killing 144 people, including 116 children

1969

21 June *Royal Family* documentary film broadcast

1 July Investiture of Prince Charles as Prince of Wales, Caernarfon Castle

1970

18 June Conservative Party led by Edward Heath elected

1972

24 February Civil List Act implements recommendations of the Select Committee on the Civil List for reform of payments and allowances to the royal family

28 May The Duke of Windsor dies in Paris

20 November Silver wedding anniversary of the Queen and the Duke of Edinburgh marked by a Thanksgiving Service in Westminster Abbey

1973

1 January Britain enters the European Economic Community

14 November Marriage of Princess Anne and Lieutenant Mark Phillips in Westminster Abbey

1974

28 February Harold Wilson and the Labour Party form a minority government. Another election on 10 October gives them a slim majority

1976

16 March Harold Wilson resigns and is replaced by James Callaghan as prime minister

1977

January–June Prince Andrew spends six months at Lakefield College School, Ontario, Canada

7 July Thanksgiving Service in St Paul's Cathedral to mark the Silver Jubilee of the Queen's accession

15 November Birth of Peter Phillips, son of Princess Anne and Captain Mark Phillips

1978

24 May Divorce of Princess Margaret and Lord Snowdon

1979

3 May Conservative government led by Mrs Thatcher elected

1–7 August Commonwealth Conference in Lusaka, Zambia

27 August Lord Mountbatten killed by an IRA bomb in Ireland

1981

15 May Birth of Zara Phillips, daughter of Princess Anne and Captain Mark Phillips

13 June The Queen shot at during the ceremony of Trooping the Colour

29 July Marriage of the Prince of Wales and Lady Diana Spencer in St Paul's Cathedral

1982

2 April–14 June Falklands War

21 June Birth of Prince William, son of the Prince and Princess of Wales

9 July Michael Fagan climbs into Buckingham Palace and enters the Queen's bedroom

September Prince Edward begins two terms at Wanganui Collegiate School, New Zealand

1984

15 September Birth of Prince Harry, son of the Prince and Princess of Wales

1986

20 July *Sunday Times* claims 'rift' between the Queen and Mrs Thatcher

23 July Marriage of Prince Andrew, Duke of York and Sarah Ferguson in Westminster Abbey

1987

13 June Princess Anne given the title Princess Royal

19 June Royal edition of 'It's a Knockout' programme broadcast, featuring the Princess Royal, the Duke and Duchess of York and Prince Edward

1988

8 August Birth of Princess Beatrice, daughter of the Duke and Duchess of York

1990

23 March Birth of Princess Eugenie, daughter of the Duke and Duchess of York

12 October The Civil List Order greatly increases the Civil List as part of a ten-year agreement

22 November Resignation of Margaret Thatcher as prime minister. She is replaced by John Major

1992

19 March Separation of the Duke and Duchess of York announced

23 April Divorce of the Princess Royal and Mark Phillips

22 June Publication of *Diana, Her True Story* by Andrew Morton

20 November Windsor Castle fire

24 November The Queen gives a speech at Guildhall to mark the 40th anniversary of her accession. She refers to recent events as part of an *annus horribilis*

26 November Announcement that the Queen will pay income tax

9 December Separation of the Prince and Princess of Wales announced

12 December The Princess Royal marries Commander Timothy Lawrence, Crathie Church, near Balmoral

1993

7 August Buckingham Palace opens to the public for the first time

8 October Marriage of Viscount Linley and the Hon. Serena Stanhope

1994

14 July Marriage of Lady Sarah Armstrong-Jones and Daniel Chatto

1995

19–25 March The Queen visits South Africa and is greeted by President Mandela. Her first visit for forty-eight years and her first as Head of State. The visit also celebrates the return of South Africa to the Commonwealth after an absence of thirty-two years

20 November Martin Bashir's controversial interview with Princess Diana for the BBC's 'Panorama' programme is aired

1996

30 May Divorce of the Duke and Duchess of York

28 August Divorce of the Prince and Princess of Wales

1997

1 May Labour government led by Tony Blair elected

31 August Death of Diana, Princess of Wales in a car accident in Paris

20 November Golden wedding anniversary of the Queen and the Duke of Edinburgh marked by a Thanksgiving Service in Westminster Abbey

11 December HMY *Britannia* decommissioned

1999

21 June Marriage of Prince Edward, Earl of Wessex and Sophie Rhys-Jones in St George's Chapel, Windsor

2000

4 August Queen Elizabeth the Queen Mother celebrates her 100th birthday

2001

11 September Terrorist attacks on the Pentagon in Washington, DC, and the World Trade Center in New York

2002

9 February Death of Princess Margaret

30 March Death of Queen Elizabeth the Queen Mother

June Golden Jubilee celebrated with a National Service of Thanksgiving at St Paul's Cathedral and the Prom at the Palace and the Party at the Palace

2003

8 November Birth of Lady Louise Windsor, daughter of the Earl and Countess of Wessex

2005

9 April Marriage of the Prince of Wales and Camilla Parker Bowles at Windsor Guildhall

2007

27 June Gordon Brown succeeds Tony Blair as prime minister

17 December Birth of James, Viscount Severn, son of the Earl and Countess of Wessex

2008

17 May Marriage of Peter Phillips and Autumn Kelly in St George's Chapel, Windsor

2009

28 November Rwanda is admitted to the Commonwealth as the fifty-fourth member

2010

17–19 January Prince William visits New Zealand on his first foreign tour representing the Queen

11 May Conservative David Cameron becomes prime minister, having formed a coalition government with the Liberal Democrats

20 October Abolition of the Civil List announced by Chancellor of the Exchequer George Osborne

2011

29 April Prince William and Catherine Middleton marry at Westminster Abbey, becoming the Duke and Duchess of Cambridge

17–20 May Queen makes historic state visit to the Republic of Ireland, the first by a British monarch since 1911

30 July Marriage of Zara Phillips and Mike Tindall at the Canongate Kirk in Edinburgh, Scotland

2012

1 April Sovereign Grant Act comes into force, replacing the Civil List

5 June Service of Thanksgiving to mark the Diamond Jubilee held at St Paul's Cathedral

27 July Opening ceremony of the Olympic Games in London

2013

22 July Birth of Prince George, son of the Duke and Duchess of Cambridge

2014

17 January Birth of Mia, daughter of Zara and Mike Tindall

2015

2 May Birth of Princess Charlotte, daughter of the Duke and Duchess of Cambridge

9 September The Queen becomes the longest-reigning British monarch

2016

23 June UK votes to leave the European Union. David Cameron resigns as prime minister the next day

13 July Theresa May becomes prime minister

2017

4 May Palace announces that Prince Philip will step down from royal duties

20 November The Queen and Prince Philip celebrate their seventieth wedding anniversary

2018

20 April Prince Charles announced as future Head of the Commonwealth

23 April Birth of Prince Louis, son of the Duke and Duchess of Cambridge

19 May Prince Harry and Meghan Markle marry in St George's Chapel, Windsor, becoming the Duke and Duchess of Sussex

18 June Birth of Lena, daughter of Zara and Mike Tindall

12 October Marriage of Princess Eugenie and Jack Brooksbank at St George's Chapel, Windsor

2019

6 May Birth of Archie, son of the Duke and Duchess of Sussex

24 July Conservative Boris Johnson becomes prime minister

2020

8 January The Duke and Duchess of Sussex announce that they will step back as senior royals

23 March Prime Minister Boris Johnson announces first UK lockdown in response to the COVID-19 pandemic

17 July Marriage of Princess Beatrice and Edoardo Mapelli Mozzi at the Royal Chapel of All Saints, Windsor

2021

9 February Birth of August, son of Princess Eugenie and Jack Brooksbank

21 March Birth of Lucas, son of Zara and Mike Tindall

9 April Death of Prince Philip, Duke of Edinburgh, aged ninety-nine

4 June Birth of Lilibet, daughter of the Duke and Duchess of Sussex

18 September Birth of Sienna, daughter of Princess Beatrice and Edoardo Mapelli Mozzi

2022

3 June Thanksgiving Service held at St Paul's Cathedral, part of a four-day series of events to celebrate the Platinum Jubilee

6 September Conservative Liz Truss becomes prime minister, the last prime minister to serve under the Queen

8 September Death of the Queen, aged ninety-six, at Balmoral, Scotland

19 September State funeral held at Westminster Abbey, followed by a private burial at St George's Chapel, Windsor

The Photographers

Bryan Adams (b. 1959)

Well-known Canadian singer, songwriter and guitarist as well as photographer. Since the 1990s Adams has conducted his photography and music careers in tandem. His sitters have been fellow rock stars, politicians, actors and royalty, including Amy Winehouse and Renée Zellweger. His photographs have been published and exhibited worldwide and the proceeds used to fund the Bryan Adams Foundation, which was established to support the most vulnerable or disadvantaged individuals in society, particularly children.

Marcus Adams (1875–1959)

Adams was the second of three generations of photographers. By the age of twenty-one he was said to be as skilled as his father, Walton Adams (1842–1934), whose sitters included Queen Victoria and King Leopold of the Belgians. Marcus Adams moved from Reading to London and established his own reputation as a photographer of children. In 1919 he joined Bertram Park and his wife Yvonne Gregory to form the 'Three Photographers', maintaining his own studio but sharing printing, retouching and darkroom staff. In 1926 Adams took the first official photographs of the then Duchess of York and her daughter Princess Elizabeth. His last royal sitting was in 1956 with Princess Anne. His son Gilbert Adams (1906–96) was apprenticed to his father and later established his own successful career.

Prince Andrew, Duke of York (b. 1960)

The Queen's second son, Prince Andrew was created Duke of York upon his marriage to Sarah Ferguson in 1986. He joined the Royal Navy in 1979 and served for twenty-two years, seeing combat as a helicopter pilot during the Falklands War. In the early 1980s the Duke became seriously interested in photography and worked with Gene Nocon, an American expert in darkroom techniques. In addition to his photographs of the Queen, his images of a number of British castles appeared on a series of postage stamps.

Godfrey Argent (1937–2006)

Argent joined the Household Cavalry in 1954 and while in the army his interest in photography began to develop; in 1960 he won the British Army Photographic Competition. In 1963 he left the army and took up photography full time. A recommendation from Field Marshal Sir Gerald Templer in due course led to the book *The Queen Rides* (1965) about the Queen and her horses. Argent later became the official photographer to the Royal Society and the National Portrait Gallery.

Brian Aris (b. 1946)

Aris began his career as a photojournalist covering the civil unrest in Northern Ireland and wars in Vietnam and the Middle East. After ten years of reportage, he opened his first studio in London and began to photograph models and friends in the music business, including David Bowie, Spandau Ballet, Boy George, Kate Bush and Bob Geldof. It was Geldof who commissioned Aris to take the now famous Band Aid group pictures. His studio work expanded to cover actors, authors, politicians and members of the royal family. Aris also took the official wedding pictures of Bob Geldof and Paula Yates, Sting and Trudie Styler, and David and Victoria Beckham, among others.

Baron (1906–56)

Baron's real name was Sterling Henry Nahum and he was brought up in Manchester, the son of an immigrant from Tripoli. Through a meeting in Malta with Lord Mountbatten he was introduced to the royal family and became a personal friend of the Duke of Edinburgh. He established a reputation as a dance, film and celebrity photographer; many of his ballet images were published in a book entitled *Baron at the Ballet* (1950). He also took many photographs of debutantes; his appointments book was said to read like a supplement to Debrett's. His style of photographs involved a lot of retouching and the colour prints were hand-tinted. He died suddenly following an operation.

Bassano

This famous West End photographic studio was founded by the photographer Alexander Bassano (1829–1913), whose subjects included Queen Victoria, Gladstone and Kitchener. His photograph of the hero of Khartoum was used for the famous recruiting poster in the First World War: 'Your Country Needs You'. Bassano retired in about 1903, when the company was relaunched as Bassano Ltd, Royal Photographers. The firm was subsequently resold on many occasions but continued to obtain royal commissions.

Cecil Beaton (1904–80)

Beaton made his name as a photographer through portraits of the Sitwells but he also worked in the world of fashion and was employed by *Vogue* and *Vanity Fair* from the late 1920s onwards. He photographed the Duke of Windsor's wedding in 1937 and in 1939 took a celebrated sequence of photographs of Queen Elizabeth at Buckingham Palace. It was said to be her influence that led to the choice of Beaton for the Coronation photographs in 1953. In response to the fashions of the times, Beaton's style of royal photograph changed from romantic images with fairy-tale backdrops in the 1940s to the use of plain backgrounds and simpler clothes in the 1960s. Post-war he became an award-winning costume and set designer, creating the costumes for the stage and film versions of *My Fair Lady*. Six volumes of his diaries were published during his lifetime. He was knighted in 1972.

Jason Bell (b. 1969)

Born in London, Bell was given his first camera at the age of five and decided to pursue a career in photography while studying at Oxford University. His work has appeared in magazines such as *Vanity Fair* and *Vogue*, and he has photographed many of Hollywood's most famous faces, including Angelina Jolie, Leonardo DiCaprio, Nicole Kidman and Daniel Craig. He has also shot film, theatre and TV campaigns for *The Crown* (Netflix), *The Rings of Power* (Amazon), *Billy Elliot* and *Love Actually*, among others. Bell was awarded Honorary Fellowships by the Royal Photographic Society and the British Institute of Professional Photography in 2011 and 2018 respectively.

Polly Borland (b. 1959)

Born in Melbourne, Australia, Borland moved to England in 1989. She is known not only for her vivid and colourful portraits but also for her less conventional subjects, such as the photographs of fetishists who dress up as babies, which led to the book *The Babies* (2001), and *Bunny* (2008), a surreal visual portrait of the English actress Gwendoline Christie.

Jane Bown (1925–2014)

Bown first worked for the *Observer* in January 1949, when the newspaper published her portrait of Bertrand Russell. This was the beginning of a career that saw her photograph many of the world's leading personalities, including Orson Welles, John Lennon, Richard Nixon, Samuel Beckett and Francis Bacon. She was known for working quickly and unobtrusively, and mostly shot in black and white using natural light. Her books include *The Gentle Eye* (1980), which was accompanied by a major exhibition at the National Portrait Gallery, London, and *Exposures* (2009).

Anthony Buckley (1912–93)

Buckley opened his first studio in 1937 and almost immediately became known for his portraits of the leading actresses of the period. After wartime service, his reputation as a leading stage portraitist increased and his subjects included Kenneth Williams, Alec Guinness and Virginia McKenna. His theatrical work also extended to production pictures for musicals. In the 1960s and 1970s he became well known as a royal photographer and received a Royal Warrant in 1963.

Julian Calder (b. 1945)

Although well known for his portraits of the royal family, Calder has photographed a broad range of subjects over his forty-year career, from artists and writers to the Masters of Livery Companies, members of the military and captains of industry. Having specialized in business photography for several years, he counts many of the largest UK companies and international corporations as clients. Calder's work has appeared in major magazines around the world, and he has also published a number of books, including *Queen's in their Name* (2021).

Lionel Cherruault (b. 1959)

Cherruault started as a photographer at Camera Press in 1979, covering a variety of subjects, including features and news. He went on to specialize in photographing the British royal family, was accredited by Buckingham Palace and covered a large number of royal tours until 1998. He now owns a family portrait studio in London.

Anthony Crickmay (1937–2020)

Crickmay began packaging parcels for photographer Lotte Meitner-Graf. In 1958 he decided to try freelancing and he went on to build a reputation as a photographer of theatre, opera, portraits (including many members of the royal family and a prime minister), fashion and particularly dance. He worked internationally and in 2017 the Victoria and Albert Theatre Museum held an exhibition of his work to mark his eightieth birthday.

Henry Dallal (b. 1955)

London-based Dallal was born in the Iranian capital of Tehran. His father gave him his first camera, a Box Brownie, as a child, and he has been taking pictures ever since, with a focus on equine pageantry and global landscapes. He took his first picture of the Queen in 2002 and photographed her regularly in her later years. His last portrait of the Queen – a print of which now hangs in the National Portrait Gallery, London – was released to mark her ninety-sixth birthday. Dallal has published more than ten books, and his work has featured in exhibitions at the Smithsonian (Washington, DC), the Royal Geographical Society (London) and the Naples Museum of Art (Florida).

Peter Grugeon (1918–80)

Grugeon was a civil servant before he opened a 'high street' photographic studio in Reading. In 1975, when the Palace needed a photographer at relatively short notice, the Secretary of the Royal Photographic Society recommended Grugeon. He was surprised to be approached but went on to take the official portraits for the Queen's Silver Jubilee in 1977. One of those photographs was used as the basis for the image of the Queen on banknotes in the Isle of Man, New Zealand and some countries in the Caribbean. The Peter Grugeon Photography Award was established in his memory.

Matt Holyoak (b. 1975)

Holyoak is renowned worldwide for his captivating portraiture. His life, he says, has been enriched by photographing many remarkable people with powerful stories, including monarchs, pioneers, artists, Olympians, freedom fighters and musicians. He has developed a visual style and aesthetic of strength and elegance, with his work featuring in *Vanity Fair*, *Vogue* and *Rolling Stone*, among others. Since 2018 he has been the official photographer for the BAFTA film awards, celebrating the achievements of top actors and filmmakers through portraiture. He was commissioned to take the official portraits for the Queen and Prince Philip's platinum wedding anniversary in 2017 and for Prince Louis of Cambridge's christening in 2018.

Yousuf Karsh (1908–2002)
Karsh was born in Turkish Armenia and emigrated to Canada when he was fifteen. After learning photography from his uncle, and an apprenticeship with John Garo in Boston, he established himself in Ottawa in the early 1930s. It was his photograph of Winston Churchill, taken there in 1941, that made his reputation. During the long and distinguished career that followed, he photographed the people who shaped the history of the last century: world leaders (including twelve US Presidents) and distinguished members of the worlds of science, art and philosophy, as well as Hollywood icons. Karsh photographed the Queen five times: from Princess to grandmother. He published many books of his portraits and an autobiography, *In Search of Greatness* (1963). He closed his studio in 1992.

Dmitri Kasterine (b. 1932)
The son of an English mother and a White Russian father, Kasterine was born in England but is now based in New York. He became a photographer after spells in the wine trade, racing cars and flying aeroplanes. He works mainly in the field of portraiture although earlier in his career he shot stills for films, notably for Stanley Kubrick on *Clockwork Orange*, *Dr Strangelove* and *The Shining*. He has worked for *Vogue*, *Vanity Fair*, the *New York Times* and *The Times* and his subjects include Samuel Beckett, Martin Amis, David Hockney and Steve Martin.

Lord Lichfield (1939–2005)
A former Guards officer, Lord Lichfield (Patrick Lichfield was his professional name) worked as assistant to Dmitri Kasterine before establishing his reputation as a chronicler of the Swinging Sixties. His biggest break came when Diana Vreeland gave him a five-year contract with American *Vogue*, where his subjects included Marsha Hunt and Michael Caine. His mother was a niece of Queen Elizabeth the Queen Mother and this gave Lord Lichfield direct access to the royal family; his most famous royal commission was the wedding of the Prince of Wales in 1981. In a career spanning more than forty years, Lord Lichfield worked on advertising commissions across several industries and published many books on photography.

Ian Leslie Macdonald
Macdonald lives in Toronto and is the regimental photographer of the 48th Highlanders of Canada. In 2017 he was invited to do a series of portraits of the Queen to celebrate her seventieth anniversary as Colonel-in-Chief of the regiment. The official portrait was released on 1 July 2017 to commemorate Canada's 150th Anniversary of Confederation. Macdonald's work has appeared in books, documentary films and magazines, and in 2019 Canada Post issued a First Day Cover featuring two of his portraits of the Queen.

Donald McKague
McKague is in the long tradition of distinguished Canadian photographers who have taken portraits of the Queen, including Karsh of Ottawa and Bryan Adams. McKague was the chosen Canadian photographer at the Coronation in 1953 and took photographs of the Queen and the Duke of Edinburgh in 1958 for the royal tour of Canada the following year.

Ranald Mackechnie (b. 1960)
British-born Mackechnie first photographed the Queen in 2013, when he was asked to provide reference shots for a painting by artist Nicky Philipps. He went on to photograph the monarch and other members of the royal family on several occasions. A previously unseen image of the Queen, taken at the same time as Mackechnie's official Platinum Jubilee portrait, was released by Buckingham Palace on the eve of her funeral. Mackechnie is also known for his photographs of professional footballers such as David Beckham and Wayne Rooney.

Robin Matthews (b. 1962)
Matthews assisted Lord Snowdon for three and a half years before he set up on his own, initially working mainly for publications such as *Tatler*, the *Telegraph* magazine and the *Sunday Times*. His work now also covers advertising and publishing. The Duchess of York's *Travels with Queen Victoria* (1993) and the *What Not to Wear* series by Trinny Woodall and Susannah Constantine are among the books that have been illustrated with Matthews's photographs.

Terry O'Neill (1938–2019)
Born in the East End of London, O'Neill wanted to be a jazz drummer. A job with BOAC's photographic unit led to a chance shot of the Home Secretary Rab Butler asleep at London airport in 1959. This was the beginning of O'Neill's spectacular career as a photographer. During the 1960s his reputation was established when he chronicled some of the most famous figures of the time, including the Beatles, Rolling Stones, Twiggy and Brigitte Bardot. Over a long and varied career his subjects included musicians, models and particularly film stars. He was married to Faye Dunaway during the 1980s.

Rankin (b. 1966)
A publisher and film director as well as a photographer, Rankin (John Rankin Waddell) first made a name for himself when he launched the style magazine *Dazed & Confused* in 1991. Since then he has portrayed many of the leading figures from the world of entertainment, including Kylie Minogue, Madonna, Jay-Z and the Rolling Stones,

and he has maintained his reputation as a cutting-edge photographer. Rankin has also tackled social issues, such as domestic violence, through his photography and has photographed campaigns for leading charities, including the Special Olympics and the Teenage Cancer Trust.

James Reid (1905–74)
Reid was a photographer with a business at Ballater, near Balmoral, specializing in pictures of children, and worked for the *Press and Journal* in Aberdeen. He was invited to Balmoral on more than one occasion in the 1950s to take photographs of the Queen and the Duke of Edinburgh with their young children.

David Secombe (b. 1962)
The son of the entertainer Harry Secombe, he has been a freelance photographer since 1986. He has worked for a wide variety of clients, including BBC Books, Time Life, the *Sunday Times* and *Telegraph* magazines, as well as organizations such as the Royal Collection and the Metropolitan Police. His sitters include Michael Bentine, Vivienne Westwood and Terry Waite.

Sir Geoffrey Shakerley (1932–2012)
Shakerley was well known for his photographs of society weddings, including those of younger members of the royal family: Prince Edward and Sophie Rhys-Jones in 1999 and Peter Phillips and Autumn Kelly in 2008. Princess Anne was a bridesmaid at Shakerley's own marriage in 1972 to Lady Elizabeth Anson, a cousin of the Queen and sister of Lord Lichfield.

Lisa Sheridan (1893–1966)
In partnership with her husband, James, Sheridan established a photographic business called Studio Lisa. He was a capable technician and she had a gift for composition and their informal photographs of family life led to an invitation to photograph the Duke and Duchess of York and the two princesses in 1936. This was the beginning of an association with the royal family that lasted to Sheridan's death; Studio Lisa held Royal Warrants from both the Queen and Queen Elizabeth the Queen Mother. Sheridan published many books of her photographs of the royal family and her autobiography, *From Cabbages to Kings*, was published in 1955.

Lord Snowdon (1930–2017)
After studying architecture at Cambridge, Antony Armstrong-Jones worked briefly for Baron before establishing his reputation by the informality he brought to society photographs. His first royal assignment was in 1957 and in 1960 he married Princess Margaret, the Queen's sister, and was created Earl of Snowdon the following year. Although divorced from the Princess in 1978, Snowdon continued to take royal photographs. His subject matter was wide-ranging but he is best known for his portraits and in 2000 the National Portrait Gallery in London held an exhibition of his work, 'Photographs by Snowdon: A Retrospective'. He was also known as the co-designer of the aviary at London Zoo and for the design work he did for the Investiture of the Prince of Wales at Caernarfon in 1969.

John Swannell (b. 1946)
Swannell assisted David Bailey for four years before setting up his own studio. He has worked extensively for magazines such as *Vogue*, *Harpers & Queen*, the *Sunday Times* and *Tatler*. In 1996–97 the National Portrait Gallery in London held an exhibition of his portraits in conjunction with the publication of his book *Twenty Years On*. Swannell has taken photographs of many members of the royal family, including the Princess Royal for her fortieth and fiftieth birthdays, Queen Elizabeth the Queen Mother for her one hundredth birthday and the Queen for the Golden and Diamond Jubilees.

Albert Watson (b. 1942)
Born in Scotland, Watson began his career in 1970 and went on to become one of the world's most successful and prolific imagemakers, blending art, fashion and commercial photography. His work has appeared on more than one hundred covers of *Vogue* worldwide and in countless other magazines including *Rolling Stone* and *Time*. He has won numerous honours and, in 2015, was awarded an OBE for his contribution to photography.

Dorothy Wilding (1893–1976)
Wilding established her own photographic studio when she was just twenty-one and by the late 1920s her Bond Street studio was attracting the leading personalities of the day. In 1937 she was invited to take the official photographs for the Coronation of George VI and in 1943 became the first woman to hold a Royal Warrant for photography. She was known for her brightly lit compositions set against a white background and many of the photographs she took of the Queen on her accession in 1952 are in this style. Her autobiography, *In Pursuit of Perfection*, was published in 1958, the year she sold her studio. In 1991 the National Portrait Gallery, London, held a retrospective exhibition of her work.

Ronald Woolf (1930–87)
Born in London, Woolf went to New Zealand when he was seven. From the 1960s he had a thriving studio in Wellington, New Zealand, and was known for his photographs of landscapes and people. He was invited to take portraits of the Queen and the Duke of Edinburgh in New Zealand in 1986. After his death in a helicopter crash in 1987, his family established the Ronald Woolf Memorial Trust to aid young New Zealand photographers. Woolf's son Simon continues the family business in Wellington. In 2010 the studio was invited to take the official photographs of Prince William's visit to New Zealand.

Index

Page numbers in *italic* refer to captions

145 Piccadilly 18–19, 36
48th Highlanders of Canada 257

Abdullah, King of Saudi Arabia 246
Adams, Bryan 234
Adams, Marcus 14, 17, 26, 27, 29, 31, 36, 41, 62, 110
Adams, Walton 27
Afghanistan 223
Albert, Prince Consort 13–14
Alexandra, Princess 164
Alexandra, Queen 155
Altrincham, Lord (John Grigg) 88, 90
Amies, Hardy 132, 159
Andrew, Prince, of Greece 22
Anne, Princess Royal 24, 66, 68, 77, 83, 90, 93, 110, 124, 128, 138, 164, 187, 188, 192, 212, 247
Argent, Godfrey 146
Aris, Brian 212, 215, 226
Armstrong-Jones, Lady Sarah, *see* Chatto, Lady Sarah
Armstrong-Jones, Sir Robert 138
Athlone, Princess Alice, Countess of 53
Australia
    1927 visit by Duke and Duchess of York 19, 26; planned 1952 visit 25; 1954 visit 88, 106; 1973 visit 190; 2002 visit 222
Auxiliary Territorial Service (ATS) 7, 21, 21, 24, 47

Balmoral Castle 19, 77, 83, 92, 146, 167, 170, 171, 172, 184, 192, 209, 218, 220, 247, 250, 252
Baron (Sterling Henry Nahum) 8, 53, 56, 60, 62, 65, 66, 73, 75, 79, 98, 100, 106, 116
Bassano, Alexander 33, 53
Bassano studio 33
BBC (British Broadcasting Corporation) 12
Beaton, Cecil 6, 7, 14, 15, 42, 44, 49, 56, 57, 58, 102, 105, 110, 113, 115, 138, 148, 156, 159, 160, 230
Bell, Jason 8, 252
Benn, Anthony Wedgwood (Tony) 92
Bennett, Tony 221
Bhumibol, King, of Thailand 221, 246
Blair, Tony 220, 222, 223
Blau, Tom 6, 8
Borland, Polly 217
Bown, Jane 240
Britannia (royal yacht) 88, 94, 169, 172, 220, 220
Brooke, Peter 188
Brown, Gordon 223
Buckingham Palace 6, 7, 8, 9, 10, 11, 12, 14, 18, 19, 20, 22, 22, 23, 36, 44, 50, 60, 66, 88, 92, 93, 95, 102, 106, 115, 116, 121, 123, 124, 132, 152, 160, 179, 183, 184, 185, 186, 187, 188, 218, 219, 219, 220, 221, 222, 224, 231, 234, 236, 242, 244
    Blue Drawing Room 113, 156, 240; Centre Room 250; Grand Staircase 98, 127, 132; Green Drawing Room 141; Music Room 50, 148; Regency Room 230; Throne Room 190, 194, 230, 257; White Drawing Room 155, 226
Buckley, Anthony 141, 152
Burrell, Paul 219–20
Butler, R.A. 89, 91

Caernarfon Castle, Gwynedd 93, 93, 240
Calder, Julian 15, 230, 245, 247, 250, 252
Camera Press 6, 7, 8
Camilla, Queen Consort (*earlier* Duchess of Cornwall) (*née* Barker Bowles) 225, 252
Canada 88, 90, 91, 155, 222
    King and Queen's 1939 visit 25; 1951 visit 25, 68; 1957 visit 75, 121; 1959 visit 90, 127, 132; 1984 visit 198, 203
Carey, Dr George (Archbishop of Canterbury) 222
Catherine, Princess of Wales (*earlier* Duchess of Cambridge) (*née* Middleton) 224, 246, 252
Cawston, Richard 92
Charles III, King (*earlier* Prince of Wales) 10, 24, 93, 183, 164, 198, 219, 220, 224, 246, 247, 252, 257
    as baby 56, 57, 60, 62; boyhood 66, 68, 83, 110, 138; education 88, 91, 93, 123; investiture 93, 93, 240; marriage to Diana 185–6, 194, 195; break-up of marriage to Diana 188–9, 218
Charteris, Martin (*later* Baron Charteris of Amisfield) 24, 25, 94, 115, 185, 186
Chatto, Daniel 228
Chatto, Lady Sarah (*née* Armstrong-Jones) 164, 228
Cherruault, Lionel 194
Churchill, Sir Winston 12, 19, 22, 25, 86, 88–9, 91
Civil List 187–8, 223–4
Clapton, Eric 221
Clarence House 4, 23–4, 65, 68, 71, 73, 252
Colville, Sir John (Jock) 24
Commonwealth 22, 23, 86, 89, 89, 90, 91, 92, 95, 105, 106, 132, 184, 222–3, 246
Connaught, Prince Arthur, Duke of 18, 42
Conservative Party 89, 91, 93, 183, 220, 223
COVID-19 pandemic 246, 247
Craig, Daniel 246
Crawford, Marion (Crawfie) 19
Crickmay, Anthony 234
Crown Estate 12, 224

Dallal, Henry 253, 260
Dazed & Confused (magazine) 239
Diana, Princess of Wales (*née* Spencer) 12, 186–9, 194, 195, 198, 218–20, 219, 224
Dimbleby, Jonathan 218

Eden, Sir Anthony 89, 91
Edward, Prince of Wales, *see* Windsor, Duke of
Edward VII, King 11
Elizabeth I, Queen 18, 24, 86, 222
Elizabeth II, Queen (*earlier* Princess)
    heir to the throne 7, 20; constitutional role 9–11, 87–9, 187; as Head of the Commonwealth 11, 88, 89, 91, 94, 184, 224; relationship with prime ministers 11, 88–9, 90–2, 95, 183–5, 220, 223, 224; royal finances 12, 94, 187–8, 223–4; walkabouts 13; State Opening of British Parliament 98, 127, 160, 190, 247; upbringing 18–19; at St Paul's Walden Bury 18, 19, 33; education 19–20; as bridesmaid 33; in Second World War 21–2, 21, 24, 38, 39, 41, 47; first radio broadcast (1940) 21; Colonel of Grenadier Guards 7, 24, 42; as Sea Ranger 42; twenty-first birthday broadcast 22–3, 183; engagement to Philip Mountbatten 22–3, 50; marriage 23, 53; early married life 23–4; accession (1952) 25, 86, 96; Coronation (1953) 7, 12, 86, 87, 102, 105, 183, 221, 224; birthday portraits 42, 44, 152, 159, 177, 190, 204, 240; attitude to Princess Margaret and Townsend 88; Christmas Day broadcast televised (1957) 88, 123; State Opening of New Zealand Parliament 152, 181; silver wedding (1972) 164, 167, 170; Silver Jubilee (1977) 12, 19, 182–3, 190; *annus horribilis* (1992) 188–9, 212; golden wedding (1997) 226; and the Millennium 221; Golden Jubilee (2002) 8, 12, 75, 217, 220, 221, 222, 230, 232, 234, 236, 239, 247; Diamond Jubilee (2012) 8, 12, 224, 246, 252; platinum wedding (2017) 246, 259; Platinum Jubilee (2022) 8, 12, 247; grandchildren/ great-grandchildren 209, 218, 246, 252
Elizabeth the Queen Mother (*earlier* Duchess of York, Queen Elizabeth) 15, 18, 18, 19, 19, 20, 20, 21, 22, 22, 25, 26, 27, 36, 38, 41, 66, 87, 164, 198, 212, 221, 245
Elphinstone, Mary Frances, Lady 18
Emirates Stadium, London 224

Fagan, Michael 187
Falkland Islands 184
Falklands Task Force 186
Fayed, Dodi Al 218
Fayed, Mohamed Al 218
Fenton, Roger 14, 14
Fisher, Dr Geoffrey (Archbishop of Canterbury) 87
France 116
Freedland, Jonathan 221

George III, King 160, 221
George IV, King 11, 121, 236
George V, King 18, 18, 19, 19, 20, 86, 145, 224, 236, 250
George VI, King (*earlier* Duke of York) 18, 18, 19, 20, 20, 22, 22, 23, 24, 25, 36, 39, 53, 60, 85, 86, 87, 236, 246, 250
George Alexander Louis, Prince 8, 246, 252, 257
Germany 159
Ghana 90–1, 91
Girl Guides 20, 42
Glamis Castle, Forfarshire 18, 19
Gordonstoun (school) 90, 91
Greville, Lady Eve 65
Grima, Andrew 259
Grugeon, Peter 177, 190
Guardian (newspaper) 221
Gunn, James 50

Hailsham, Quintin Hogg, Lord 91
Harry, Prince 198, 209, 218, 223, 252
Hartnell, Norman 49, 53, 80, 105, 116, 127, 152, 190
Heath, Edward 90, 93–5, 184, 222
Henry VIII, King 87
Heseltine, Sir William 92
Hillary, Edmund 87
Hitler, Adolf 41
Holyoak, Matt 8, 259
Home, Alec Douglas-Home, 14th Earl of 91–2

India 141, 188
IRA (Irish Republican Army) 185, 224

Iraq 223
Ireland, Republic of 185, 224–5
'It's a Knockout' (TV programme) 187

Johns Hopkins University, Baltimore 246

Karsh, Yousuf 4, 6, 14–15, 68, 71, 75, 155, 198, 203, 209, 236
Kasterine, Dmitri 179
Kaunda, Kenneth 184
Kelly, Angela 250, 252, 259
Kensington Palace 12
Kent, Katharine, Duchess of 164
Kent, Edward, Duke of 164
Kent, George, Duke of 33
Kent, Princess Marina, Duchess of 33
Kent, Prince Michael of 164
Kenya 25
Kilmuir, David Maxwell Fyfe, 1st Earl of 90
Knight, Clara ('Alla') 18, 19

Labour Party 89, 92, 94
Lamont, Norman 220
Lancaster House Agreement 184
Lascelles, George 18
Lascelles, Gerald 18
Lascelles, Princess Mary, Viscountess (later Princess Royal, Countess of Harewood) 18, 18
Lascelles, Sir Alan 10, 15
Lee Kuan Yew 184
Liberal Party 94
Libya 185
Lichfield, Patrick Anson, 5th Earl of 8, 160, 164, 167, 169, 170, 171, 172, 179, 195, 229, 236
Linley, David, Viscount 146, 164, 179, 212
Linley, Serena, Viscountess (née Stanhope) 212

McCartney, Sir Paul 221
Macdonald, Ian Leslie 257
McGuinness, Martin 224
McKague, Donald 127, 132, 134
Mackechnie, Ranald 8, 257
Macleod, Iain 91
Macmillan, Harold 89, 90, 91, 187
Major, John 187
Malta 24
Margaret Rose, Princess 8, 14, 19, 20, 20, 21, 22, 33, 39, 41, 42, 77, 87–8, 116, 138, 164, 179, 212, 221
Marten, Henry 20
Mary, Queen 18, 18, 19, 20, 65, 116, 221
Marylebone Cricket Club 12
Matthews, Robin 228
May, Brian 221
Middleton, Catherine, see Catherine, Princess of Wales
Millennium Dome, London 220–1
Mirren, Dame Helen 220
Morton, Andrew
    Diana: Her True Story (1992) 188–9
Mountbatten, Admiral Louis, 1st Earl 22, 24, 86, 89, 92, 185–6, 225
Mountbatten, Pamela 25
Mountbatten, Patricia 21

Nasser, Colonel Gamel Abdel 89
New York Herald Tribune 12
New Zealand 88, 91, 94, 181, 222
    1927 visit by Duke and Duchess of York 19, 26; planned 1952 visit 25; 1954 visit 88; 1963 visit 152; 1986 visit 181; 2002 visit 221
Nigeria 14, 115

Nizam of Hyderabad 80
Nkrumah, Kwame 90, 91
Norgay, Sherpa Tenzing 87
Northern Ireland 183, 225
Nyerere, Julius 184

Ogilvy, James 164
Ogilvy, Marina 164
Ogilvy, Sir Angus 164
Olympic Games, London (2012) 246
Olympic Games, Montreal (1976) 128
O'Neill, Terry 209, 210, 212
Order of the Garter 85, 100, 110, 116, 160, 236, 250
Osborne, George 223

Pakistan 141
Philip, Prince, Duke of Edinburgh 8, 22–5, 50, 53, 73, 75, 79, 86, 93, 98, 105, 116, 121, 127, 155, 164, 171, 183, 209, 212, 218, 219, 224, 226, 244, 246, 252, 259
Phillips, Peter 190, 192, 209
Pimlott, Ben 91, 184
Plunket, Patrick Plunket, 7th Baron 185
Ponsonby, Sir Frederick 92
Powell, Enoch 91

Queen (rock group) 221
Queen, The (film) 220

Radio Times 179
Ramphal, Sir Sonny 184
Rankin (John Rankin Waddell) 239
Reid, James 12, 77
Rhodes, Lady Margaret 224
Richard, Cliff 221
Ritz hotel (London) 223
Ritz hotel (Paris) 218
Rosse, Anne, Countess of 138
Rothschild, Lord Victor 182
Royal Collection 187
royal family 164
    British perception of 12–15, 23; relationship with press 11–12, 92
Royal Family (1969 TV film) 92, 93
Royal Lodge, Windsor 36, 38, 41
Royal Mail 196
Royal Mews 223
Royal Naval College, Dartmouth 22
Royal Photographic Society 14
Royal Warrant 42, 142
Runcie, Robert (Archbishop of Canterbury) 186, 194

Salisbury, Robert Gascoyne-Cecil, 5th Marquess of 90
Sandringham House, Norfolk 25, 123, 146, 204, 209, 212, 223, 232
Secombe, David 230
Secombe, Harry 230
Serres, Dominic 160
Shakerley, Sir Geoffrey 229
Shea, Michael 185
Sheridan, Lisa, see Studio Lisa
Simpson, Mrs Wallis (later Wallis, Duchess of Windsor) 11, 20
Smith, Ian 92
Snowdon, Antony Armstrong-Jones, 1st Earl of 6, 8, 88, 116, 121, 123, 124, 127, 138, 160, 164, 190, 196, 226, 240, 242
South Africa 22–3, 80, 90, 183
Southern Rhodesia (later Zimbabwe) 92, 184
Sovereign Grant Act 12, 224

Spencer, Lady Diana, see Diana, Princess of Wales
Stark, Koo 186
St Andrews, George Windsor, Earl of 164
St Margaret's, Westminster 212
St Paul's Cathedral 19, 182–3, 222
St Paul's Walden Bury, Hertfordshire 18, 19, 33
Strathmore and Kinghorne, Cecilia Nina, Countess of 18, 18, 19
Strathmore and Kinghorne, Claude George Bowes Lyon, 14th Earl of 18, 18, 19
Studio Lisa (Lisa Sheridan, James Sheridan) 36, 38, 39, 83, 128, 137, 142, 144, 145, 150, 152
Suez Crisis (1956) 89–90
Sunday Times 185
Sunninghill Park, Berkshire 23, 186
Swannell, John 236, 250

Thatcher, Margaret 183–5, 187, 222
Tindall, Zara (née Phillips) 209
Times, The 185
Townsend, Group Captain Peter 87–8
Trooping the Colour 9, 24, 187
Truman, Harry S. 25
Truss, Liz 247

United States of America 14, 25, 53, 222

VE Day 22, 22
Vladimir, Maria Pavlovna, Grand Duchess 116, 132
Victoria, Queen 11, 13–14, 14, 18, 22, 27, 132, 172, 182, 221, 246, 250, 252

Washington Evening Star 25
Watson, Albert 204
Weber, Max 13
Welby, Justin (Archbishop of Canterbury) 247
Wessex, Prince Edward, Earl of 90, 91, 148, 150, 164, 186–7, 229
Wessex, Sophie, Countess of (née Rhys-Jones) 229
Westminster Abbey 23, 87, 87, 102, 105, 224, 234
Westminster Hall 221
Wilding, Dorothy 7, 14, 15, 20, 21, 42, 47, 50, 80, 85, 96
William, Prince of Wales (earlier Duke of Cambridge) 198, 209, 218, 224, 246, 252, 257
Wilson, Harold 11, 92–5
Windlesham Moor, Surrey 23
Windsor, Edward, Duke of (earlier Prince of Wales, King Edward VIII) 7, 11, 18, 19, 20
Windsor, Lady Helen 164
Windsor, Lord Nicholas 164
Windsor Castle 9, 19, 21, 22, 41, 44, 128, 142, 144, 145, 145, 150, 152, 177, 198, 228, 236, 246, 247, 252, 257
    1992 fire 188, 188
Windsor Great Park 23
Windsor Home Park 137
Woolf, Ronald 181

York, Prince Andrew, Duke of 90, 91, 144, 145, 146, 148, 150, 164, 184, 186–7, 188, 204, 232
York, Sarah, Duchess of (née Ferguson) 186–7, 188, 204
Young, Hugo 183

Zambia 184

Acknowledgments

This book grew out of the exhibition 'Elizabeth II and Camera Press: 60 Years of a Gentleman's Agreement' at the 2007 Rencontres d'Arles photography festival, curated by François Hebel.

I would like to thank my colleagues at Camera Press for their invaluable assistance, particularly Jacqui Wald and the late Donald Chapman whose extensive and thorough research was of immense help. I am also indebted to the co-operation and enthusiasm of the photographers, their offices and estates; the book would not have been possible without them.

The staff at Thames & Hudson have been passionate about the book from the very beginning and I thank them for all their hard work.

Finally, I would like to express my gratitude to both the Buckingham Palace press office and the Royal Collection for all the help given by their staff.

Emma Blau

By gracious permission of Her Majesty the Queen I was allowed to read and quote from certain letters in the Royal Archives at Windsor relating to the royal family and official royal photographers.

I must express my obligation to the two leading biographers of Queen Elizabeth II, Mrs Sarah Bradford and the late Professor Ben Pimlott, whose works I have found of the greatest value in writing this book.

Philip Ziegler

About the Authors

Philip Ziegler is the bestselling author of *Mountbatten: The Official Biography*, *King Edward VIII: The Official Biography*, *Diana Cooper: The Biography of Lady Diana Cooper* and *London at War, 1939–1945*.

Emma Blau FRSA is an award-winning photographic artist, curator and commentator. She is co-owner of Camera Press, the photo agency founded by her grandfather that hosts the work of royal photographers from throughout the Queen's life. She directed and produced the documentary *Camera Press at 70: A Lifetime in Pictures*. Her photography is held in the collection of the National Portrait Gallery, London, and the Parliamentary Art Collection, UK.

Credits

All photographs are © Camera Press and the photographer named in the caption unless otherwise stated below.

All Patrick Lichfield photographs are © Lichfield Archive/ Getty Images.

p. 13 © Camera Press/Illustrated London News
p. 19 © Camera Press/Illustrated London News
p. 21 © Camera Press/Imperial War Museum
p. 22 © Camera Press/Imperial War Museum
p. 87 © Camera Press/Tom Blau
p. 89 © Camera Press/Pix Sydney
p. 91 © Camera Press/H/D
p. 93 above © Camera Press/Joan Williams
p. 93 below © Camera Press
pp. 209–212 © Terry O'Neill/Iconic Images
p. 222 © Camera Press/Richard Open

The author and publishers acknowledge the following sources of quotations:

Cecil Beaton from *Cecil Beaton: The Royal Portraits* by Roy Strong (Thames & Hudson, London, 1988)

Lisa Sheridan from *Our Princesses At Home* (John Murray, London, 1940) and *From Cabbages to Kings* (Odhams Press, London, 1955), both by Lisa Sheridan